ROMANTIC
ITALIAN COOKING
AUTHENTIC RECIPES JUST FOR TWO

CONTENTS

ANOTHER BEST-SELLING VOLUME FROM HPBooks®
Publisher: Rick Bailey
Editorial Director: Elaine R. Woodard
Editor: Jeanette P. Egan; Art Director: Don Burton
Book Assembly: Leslie Sinclair
Typography: Cindy Coatsworth, Michelle Carter
Director of Manufacturing: Anthony B. Narducci

Published by HPBooks, Inc.
P.O. Box 5367, Tucson, AZ 85703   602/888-2150
ISBN 0-89586-395-2
Library of Congress Catalog Card Number 85-81328
©1986 HPBooks, Inc. Printed in the U.S.A.
1st Printing

Originally published as Romantic Italian Cookery
©1985 Hennerwood Publications Limited

Cover Photo: Veal with Tuna Mayonnaise, page 42

As restaurant eating becomes increasingly expensive, entertaining at home grows in popularity. There are other advantages besides economy: It is easier to relax and talk in your own home. There are no neighbors to listen in on conversations or waiters to interrupt. And there's no rush to leave your table at the end of the meal!

CHOOSING THE MENU

The first step in planning a romantic dinner for two is to decide on a menu. The menu should suit your taste and that of your dinner partner and set the mood you wish to create. The amount of preparation involved and your budget need to be considered also.

The menu itself can be as simple or elaborate as you wish. Avoid too many recipes that require last-minute preparation. The more you can prepare ahead, the more relaxed and confident you will feel. Check equipment; don't overload your oven or plan menus that require special utensils.

You may want to serve only one beautifully prepared and presented main dish followed by a delicious array of fruit and cheeses. Or you might want to serve several smaller courses that provide flavor and color contrasts. You will find that many of the pasta, rice and pizza recipes, and some of the vegetables and salads, serve equally well as starters or as part of a main course. Serve smaller portions if using these as starters. Most of the vegetable recipes are generous enough to allow for second servings. Whatever you decide on, try to balance the courses so they are not too filling. For example, if you choose a pasta starter, offer a light main course. Serve a more substantial main dish after a vegetable or salad starter.

Here is a menu suggestion with balance in flavor, color and texture.

Ham with Avocado, page 19
Stuffed Chicken Breasts, page 52
Rice Pilaf with Mushrooms, page 26
Tossed Green Salad
Strawberry Ice, page 74
Cheese Board
Coffee

In this menu the main dish, salad and dessert can be prepared several hours ahead. The rice is quick to cook and needs little attention. The pink and green starter contrasts with the lighter colored main course. The dessert provides a fresh taste to round off the meal. The cheese board is optional.

PLANNING

A good suggestion for preparing a meal is to have a written plan. Write down when to start each dish and how long it takes to cook. Note times that food must be re-moved from oven or freezer. Also allow time between each course. Write the times as a countdown. Put your work plan in an easy-to-read place in the kitchen. Remember to give yourself plenty of time to set the table. If your dinner partner enjoys cooking, he or she may want to help.

If possible, try to clear up as you go along. Otherwise you may find that you run out of clean saucepans and utensils. And you'll have a stack to do later. If your kitchen is small, remember that dirty dishes take up work space. If the kitchen is visible from the dining area, make it as neat as possible before serving dinner.

KEEPING FOOD WARM

You may want to prepare some foods ahead of time. Most of the main dishes in this book will keep warm long enough for you to enjoy the first dinner course.

Many of the main dishes can be covered tightly with a lid or foil and kept warm in a preheated 250F (120C) oven. Fish tends to dry out slightly without special attention. To prevent dryness, wrap the cooked fish in foil; place foil-wrapped fish on a rack in a roasting pan partially filled with hot water. Place in preheated oven. However, fish that has a crisp breading does not stand well without becoming soggy.

Most sauces can be partly or completely prepared before the first course; reheat over low heat before serving. A salad without dressing can be covered with plastic wrap and refrigerated for a few hours; add the dressing just before serving.

If you wish, cook pasta ahead of time. Rinse the cooked pasta with cool water; cool to room temperature. When ready to serve, place cooled pasta into boiling water; stir 1 to 2 minutes. Drain thoroughly. To prepare rice ahead, cover cooked rice with damp waxed paper; keep warm in a preheated 250F (120C) oven.

DRINKS

Have ice, aperitifs, orange slices and lemon slices on hand. Chill white wines or light red wines. Some red wines benefit from standing, uncorked, 1 to 2 hours before serving. If serving an inexpensive jug wine, pour into an attractive decanter. See page 9 for advice on Italian wines. All main dishes give a suggested type of wine.

CHEESE BOARD

An attractive and delicious cheese board need consist of only two or three delicious Italian cheeses. Unwrap cheeses; let stand at room temperature an hour or so before serving for the best flavor. The cheese can be ar-ranged on a plate or board. Garnish with a small bunch of grapes, a few watercress sprigs, orange wedges or fresh herbs. Serve with crackers in a napkin-lined basket and butter or margarine in a chilled dish.

COFFEE

Well-made coffee provides a perfect end to a meal. The Italians drink small cups of strong black *caffe espresso*, or frothy, milky *caffe cappuccino*, using a dark-roasted coffee. If you don't own a *caffettiera*, a *napoletana* or a *moka*, which are all Italian-style coffee pots, filter coffee is the nearest equivalent. Choose a blend of coffee to suit your taste, but avoid the lighter roasts. Vienna coffee and mocha blends are two worth trying. To make frothy *caffe cappuccino*, heat the milk; blend hot milk in a blender or beat with an electric mixer until frothy. Pour frothed milk into hot black coffee; sprinkle with chocolate drink mix. *Caffe corretto*, coffee laced with a liqueur or brandy, can be served with a few macaroons or thin wedges of *Panforte*, an Italian sweet.

THE COOK'S TOOLS

No special utensils are needed to prepare these recipes, but you might find the following useful:

Food processor or blender — For pureeing soups and sauces, making bread crumbs, grating cheese, chopping herbs and a thousand other little jobs.

Electric mixer — For whipping cream and egg whites, making sorbet and whisking egg yolks and sugar together.

Nutmeg grater — For grating whole nutmeg. Once you taste freshly grated nutmeg, you'll consider this tool indispensible.

Slotted spoon — For removing fried food from fat. Do not use a wire basket for food in batter, such as Deep-Fried Veal & Vegetables, page 50; the batter tends to stick to the wire mesh.

Mortar and pestle — For crushing garlic; making green sauce and dressings; crushing spices, such as juniper berries, and mixing small quantities.

Cheese board: Clockwise from top right: Bel Paese, Gorgonzola, Fontina, Pecorino; cups of Cappuccino

SPECIAL INGREDIENTS

Italian ingredients are available in many supermarkets and delicatessens. The items listed here are ingredients used in this book or ones you might want to try. Some substitutes are suggested.

Cheeses

Bel Paese — A soft, creamy, melting cheese. Use as a table cheese and for cooking. It can be used instead of mozzarella for pizza toppings, salads and appetizers.

Fontina — A semihard cheese with a sweet, nutty flavor and creamy texture. Eat as a table cheese and use as a melting cheese in cooked dishes, such as Piedmontese Cheese Soup, page 12.

Gorgonzola — A mild, blue-veined cheese from Lombardy. *Dolcelatte* is a creamy type of Gorgonzola.

Mozzarella — A moist, waxy cheese. It is commonly used as a pizza topping although it has many other uses. It can be fried, baked and used in salads.

Parmesan (Parmigiano) — The most famous of all Italian cheeses. Parmesan is hard when aged. It is finely grated and used in countless Italian dishes. Buy ungrated Parmesan cheese at large supermarkets and delicatessens. The flavor of freshly grated Parmesan is superior to commercially grated cheese.

Pecorino — A sheep's-milk cheese that is hard when aged. It makes a good, but sharper, alternative to Parmesan. Grated, it is excellent with pasta. When fresh, pecorino is light in color and soft in texture. It makes a delicious addition to the cheese board.

Provolone — A creamy white, firm cheese. Use in cooking and for appetizers or as part of a cheese board. It is also delicious in sandwiches.

Ricotta — A soft, white, crumbly cheese. It is used for

Assorted Italian cold cuts, sausages and other ingredients

both sweet and savory dishes. It has a bland, slightly salty flavor. If you are unable to buy ricotta, use drained and sieved cottage cheese.

Romano — A pale-yellow, hard cheese. It has a sharp flavor. Grate to use in cooking.

Cured Meats & Sausages

Bresaola — Dry-cured beef fillet cut into wafer-thin slices. Serve as an antipasto. Sprinkle with olive oil, pepper and freshly squeezed lemon juice. If bresaola is not available, look for dry-cured beef fillet under other names.

Cotechin — A spicy pork sausage. Boil and serve with hot vegetables, or slice and serve cold.

Mortadella — The largest Italian cured sausage. Made with pork and spices and studded with pork fat. Serve cold in thin slices, or dice and add to cooked dishes.

Prosciutto di Parma — Delicately cured ham eaten in wafer-thin slices. Good with figs or melon. Prosciutto-style hams are available in the U.S.

Salami — There are numerous types of Italian salami. The most commonly available are *Salame milanese*, *Salame napoletana* and *Salame genovese*. These all tend to be coarse-textured and lightly seasoned. Serve a small quantity with olives as a simple antipasto.

Salsicce — Fresh meaty sausages for grilling or frying. Usually made of pork, some are peppery hot while others are only mildly flavored. There are countless names given to various types, but in Italy *Salsiccia al metro* is sold by the meter, hence its name. *Salamella* is often the same mixture tied into links with string. Another type sold in Italy is *Luganeghe*.

Herbs

Herbs play an important part in many Italian dishes. Fresh herbs have the best flavor and are becoming easier to buy. Or you can grow your own. Those most commonly used are basil, bay leaves, oregano, marjoram, parsley, rosemary and sage.

Garlic is used throughout Italy. The flavor can be modified to suit your taste, except in dishes, such as Basil Sauce (Pesto), page 13, and Garlic & Anchovy Dip (Bagna Cauda), page 16, which rely heavily on garlic flavor. Pink-skinned garlic tends to have a sweeter flavor than the white.

Mushrooms

Wild mushrooms, such as cèpes, can be bought in the autumn in some markets. They are used in sauces, rice dishes, soups, omelets and many other dishes. If fresh mushrooms are not available, substitute dried mushrooms for a rich, concentrated flavor. Soak dried mushrooms in warm water 30 minutes. Drain; thinly slice. If the imported mushrooms are not available, substitute commercially grown fresh mushrooms.

Olive Oil

In southern Italy, olive oil is used extensively for cooking. Northern Italians favor butter for cooking and in Central Italy, they use a mixture of both! Buy the best olive oil you can afford. Cheap olive oil is a false economy when it is overpowering in flavor.

Pine Nuts

These distinctive nuts are the seeds of the pine cone.

They are used in meat and game dishes, particularly in stuffings, and sweet and sour sauces. Pine nuts are very difficult to shell. Look for unshelled ones in large supermarkets and gourmet shops. Like all nuts, pine nuts are best when fresh.

Rice

Italian rice is thicker and shorter grained than long-grain rice. The texture of the cooked rice is creamy, in contrast to long-grain rice which is dry and fluffy. Use Italian arborio rice or California short-grain pearl rice. Do not use Oriental short-grain rice that has been coated with talc.

Pasta

There are as many varieties of pasta as there are ways of serving it. There's green pasta, whole-wheat pasta and even red pasta made from tomatoes or beets. Pasta is available fresh, dried and frozen. It is made in countless shapes and sizes.

Dried pasta will take longer to cook than fresh or frozen. Different shapes of pasta will vary in their cooking time, too. Pasta cooked al dente is firm to the bite and this is how Italians eat pasta. Check pasta by trying a small piece after the minimum cooking time; do not overcook.

To cook pasta, bring a large saucepan of salted water to a boil. Use about 4 quarts of water and 1 tablespoon salt for every 1 pound of pasta. When the water is rapidly boiling, add pasta all at once. To cook spaghetti, feed strands into the boiling water as it softens. Stir pasta with a large wooden spoon to prevent sticking. Cook uncovered. Drain cooked pasta quickly in a large colander; shake colander to remove excess water. Return drained pasta to saucepan; toss with a little butter, a little grated Parmesan cheese or both.

Tomatoes

Juicy ripe tomatoes make the best sauce. In winter or when good-tasting ripe tomatoes are not available, use canned Italian tomatoes. To thicken and enrich sauces, add the concentrated flavor of tomato paste. A pinch of sugar or honey added to tomato dishes helps to balance the flavor.

Marsala

This fortified wine is used extensively in Italian cooking. It is used for desserts and also for some savory dishes. Choose dry or medium Marsala for cooking. Avoid Marsala all'Uovo, a sweet dessert wine unsuitable for cooking.

GUIDE TO ITALIAN WINES

Each of the meat, poultry and fish recipes include a suggestion for a type of wine. Here is a selection of Italian wines which fit into each of those categories. You will find that many of the wines are available from supermarkets, wine stores and gourmet shops.

Robust Red Wines
Barbera
Barolo
Nebbiolo
Venegazzu
Brunello di Montalcino
Cabernet Grave del Fruili
Valpolicella

Light Red Wines
Raboso del Veneto
Bardolino
Lambrusco — Slightly sparkling. Ranges from sweet to dry. Serve chilled.

Dry Red Wines
Chianti Classico
Barbaresco

Fruity Medium-Dry Red Wines
Sangiovese de Romagna
Dolcetto

Fruity Medium-Dry White Wine
Orvieto Abboccato

Fruity Dry White Wines
Pinot Grigio
Tocai
Verdicchio

Light Dry White Wines
Soave
Verduzzo del Piave

Dry White Wines
Orvieto
Frascati
Vernaccia

Italian Liqueurs
To round off the meal there are several Italian liqueurs to choose from:
Grappa — A fiery liqueur made from grape skins and seeds. It is usually flavored with a plant called rue.
Maraschino — A sweet liqueur made from cherries.
Strega — An herb-flavored liqueur.
Amaretto di Saronno — A strong almond-flavored liqueur.
Sambuca — An anise-flavored liqueur.

Soups & Starters

Seafood Salad

Insalata di Frutti di Mare

1/2 small red bell pepper
1 small carrot
1 celery stalk
1 small onion, thinly sliced
Lettuce leaves
4 oz. deveined, peeled, cooked shrimp
1 (3-1/2-oz.) can water-pack tuna, drained, flaked
4 pimento-stuffed green olives, sliced

Dressing:
3 tablespoons olive oil
1 tablespoon lemon juice
1 garlic clove, crushed
1 teaspoon chopped fresh marjoram or 1/2 teaspoon
    dried leaf marjoram
Salt
Freshly ground pepper

1. Cut bell pepper, carrot and celery into thin strips. In a small bowl, combine bell-pepper, carrot and celery strips and onion. Arrange lettuce leaves on 2 small plates. Arrange vegetable mixture over lettuce.
2. In a small bowl, combine shrimp, tuna and olives; spoon shrimp mixture over salad.
3. Place all dressing ingredients in a small container with a tight-fitting lid. Shake to combine. Dressing and salad can be covered and refrigerated separately up to 8 hours. If made ahead, shake dressing before serving.
4. To serve, pour dressing over salad. Makes 2 servings.

Salmon & Herb Mousse

Mousse di Salmone

2/3 (3-oz.) pkg. Neufchâtel cheese, room temperature
1 tablespoon lemon juice
1 (3-1/2-oz.) can salmon, drained, flaked
Salt
Freshly ground pepper

To serve:
2 lettuce leaves
2 tablespoons finely chopped mixed fresh herbs
    (chives, tarragon, parsley, marjoram or basil)

1. In a medium bowl, beat Neufchâtel cheese and lemon juice until smooth. Stir in salmon; season with salt and pepper. Salmon mixture can be covered and refrigerated up to 2 hours.
2. To serve, place a lettuce leaf on each of 2 plates; mound salmon mixture on each lettuce-lined plate. Sprinkle with herbs. Makes 2 servings.

Deep-Fried Paprika Sardines

Sarde Fritte

3 to 4 (2- to 3-oz.) fresh or thawed frozen sardines
    or smelt, cleaned, page 39
1/2 teaspoon salt
2 teaspoons paprika
2 teaspoons all-purpose flour
Vegetable oil

To garnish:
Lemon slices
Parsley sprigs

1. Pat fish dry with paper towels.
2. Combine salt, paprika and flour in a shallow dish. Roll fish in flour mixture until coated.
3. In a large deep saucepan, heat 3 inches of oil to 350F (175C) or until a 1-inch bread cube turns golden brown in 65 seconds.
4. Fry fish in hot oil 3 to 4 minutes or until crisp and golden brown. Drain on paper towels; serve hot. Garnish with lemon slices and parsley. Makes 2 servings.

Left to right: Deep-Fried Paprika Sardines, Seafood Salad

Piedmontese Cheese Soup

Fonduta Piemontese

1 cup milk
6 oz. fontina cheese, cut into small cubes
2 egg yolks, lightly beaten
2 tablespoons butter or margarine
2 fresh mushrooms, thinly sliced

To serve:
French bread

This cheese soup is also delicious as a fondue with French-bread cubes for dipping.

Clockwise from bottom left: Cold Minestrone with Basil Sauce, Piedmontese Cheese Soup, Tomato Soup with Herbs

1. In top of a double double over simmering water, heat milk until hot. Remove from heat; stir in cheese and egg yolks.
2. Cook over simmering water, stirring occasionally, until cheese melts and mixture is smooth. Stir in butter or margarine until melted.
3. Spoon soup into 2 soup bowls; sprinkle with mushroom slices. Serve with French bread. Makes 2 servings.

Tomato Soup with Herbs

Minestra di Pomodoro con Odori

1 tablespoon olive oil
1 small onion, finely chopped
1 small boiling potato, peeled, finely chopped
1 garlic clove, crushed
4 small tomatoes, peeled, chopped
1/2 teaspoon dried leaf oregano
1 tablespoon chopped fresh celery leaves
1/2 teaspoon dried leaf basil
Pinch of sugar
Salt
Freshly ground pepper

Croutons:
2 bread slices
1/4 cup olive oil

To garnish:
Parsley sprigs

1. Heat olive oil in a medium saucepan over medium heat. Add onion, potato and garlic; sauté 5 minutes or until onion is soft.
2. Stir in tomatoes, oregano, celery leaves and basil. Season with sugar, salt and pepper. Bring to a boil; reduce heat. Cover; simmer 15 minutes, stirring occasionally.
3. In a blender or food processor with a steel blade, process soup until pureed. Soup can be cooled, covered and refrigerated up to 24 hours.
4. Pour pureed soup into a clean saucepan. Heat until hot.
5. Make croutons while soup is heating. Using a small heart cutter or a very sharp knife, cut out 4 heart shapes from each bread slice. In a medium skillet, heat oil. Add bread hearts; sauté, turning once, until crisp and golden. Drain on paper towels.
6. To serve, pour soup into 2 soup bowls; serve hot with croutons. Garnish with parsley. Makes 2 servings.

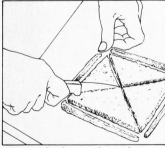 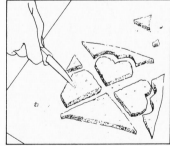

1/To make heart-shaped croutons, remove crust from bread slice. Cut trimmed bread diagonally into 4 triangles.

2/Using a small knife and starting at center of outside edge, cut out a small V as shown. Round corners to make a heart shape.

Cold Minestrone with Basil Sauce

Minestrone Freddo con Pesto

Basil Sauce (Pesto):
1 bunch fresh basil, finely chopped
2 garlic cloves, peeled
1 tablespoon finely chopped pine nuts
1/3 cup grated Parmesan cheese (1 oz.)
1/4 cup olive oil

Minestrone:
1 tablespoon olive oil
1 garlic clove, crushed
1 small eggplant, cubed
2 small tomatoes, peeled, chopped
1 medium zucchini, sliced
1 tablespoon tomato paste
1/2 cup water
Salt
Freshly ground pepper

To serve:
Grated Parmesan cheese

Served cold, this starter has a similar texture and flavor to French ratatouille. For a hearty winter soup, serve hot. Pesto is available in jars in some large supermarkets or delicatessens.

1. To make pesto, in a blender, combine basil, garlic, nuts and cheese. Process until pureed. While machine motor is running, slowly pour in olive oil. If not serving immediately, cover and refrigerate until served or up to 3 days.
2. In a medium saucepan, heat olive oil. Add garlic; sauté 1 minute.
3. Add eggplant, tomatoes and zucchini. Cover; simmer 5 minutes.
4. Stir in tomato paste and water. Season with salt and pepper. Bring to a boil, stirring. Reduce heat. Simmer about 5 minutes or until vegetables are almost tender when pierced with a fork.
5. Cool to room temperature or cover and refrigerate up to 24 hours. Bring to room temperature before serving. Pour soup mixture into soup bowls.
6. To serve, stir pesto into each bowl; sprinkle with Parmesan cheese. Makes 2 servings.

Sorrel Soup

Minestra all'Acetosa

2 tablespoons butter or margarine
1 medium onion, chopped
2 small boiling potatoes, peeled, chopped
Salt
Freshly ground pepper
1-1/2 cups chicken stock
3/4 cup shredded sorrel leaves
2 tablespoons half and half
2 teaspoons chopped chives

1. Melt butter in a medium saucepan over medium-low heat. Add onion and potatoes. Cover; cook about 10 minutes, stirring occasionally.
2. Season with salt and pepper. Stir in stock; bring to a boil. Reduce heat. Simmer, uncovered, about 5 minutes or until potatoes are tender when pierced with a fork.
3. Stir in sorrel leaves; cook 5 minutes or until tender. In a blender or food processor with a steel blade, process soup until pureed.
4. Pour pureed soup into 2 soup bowls; swirl 1 tablespoon half and half into each bowl. Sprinkle with chives. Makes 2 servings.

Variation
Watercress Soup (Zuppa di Crescione): Substitute 1 watercress bunch, trimmed and chopped, for sorrel leaves.

Spinach & Polenta Soup

Minestra di Spinaci e Polenta

1/4 cup butter or margarine
1 garlic clove, crushed
1 lb. spinach, washed, trimmed
1/8 teaspoon ground nutmeg
Salt
Freshly ground pepper
1 tablespoon cornmeal
1-1/2 cups chicken stock
1/4 cup half and half

1. Melt butter or margarine in a medium saucepan. Add garlic; sauté 1 minute.
2. Stir in spinach and nutmeg. Season with salt and pepper. Cover; cook 2 minutes. Stir in cornmeal and stock; bring to a boil
3. Reduce heat; simmer, stirring occasionally, 5 minutes or until spinach is tender. In a blender or food processor with a steel blade, process soup until pureed.
4. Rinse saucepan. Pour pureed soup into rinsed saucepan; heat just until heated through. Stir in half and half; heat until hot. Do not boil.
5. To serve, pour hot soup into 2 soup bowls. Makes 2 servings.

Chicken Soup with Marsala

Zuppa di Pollo con Marsala

1 boneless chicken-breast half, skinned
1 small carrot, chopped
1 celery stalk, chopped
2 whole cloves
1 (2-inch) cinnamon stick
1 medium onion, peeled
2 cups water
Bouquet garni
2 egg yolks
1/4 cup Marsala
2 tablespoons butter or margarine, cut into pieces
Ground nutmeg

1. In a medium saucepan, combine chicken, carrot, celery, cloves, cinnamon, onion, water and bouquet garni. Bring to a boil. Reduce heat. Cover; simmer 1 hour.
2. Strain broth into a bowl, discarding vegetables and spices. Cut chicken into thin strips; set aside. Rinse saucepan.
3. In a small bowl, combine egg yolks and Marsala. Stir egg-yolk mixture into strained broth. Strain into rinsed saucepan; cook, stirring, until almost boiling.
4. Stir in butter or margarine, a piece at a time; cook until soup is slightly thickened. Do not boil. Stir in reserved chicken; heat until hot.
5. To serve, pour soup into 2 soup bowls; sprinkle with nutmeg. Makes 2 servings.

Top to bottom: Sorrel Soup, Chicken Soup with Marsala

Left to right: Tarragon Omelet, Garlic & Anchovy Dip with raw vegetables, Spinach & Ricotta Tart

Tarragon Omelet

Frittata al Dragoncello

---

3 eggs
1 tablespoon half and half
1 tablespoon chopped fresh tarragon or 1 teaspoon
 dried leaf tarragon
Salt
Freshly ground pepper
2 tablespoons butter or margarine

To garnish:
Fresh tarragon sprigs, if desired

---

1. Preheat broiler. In a small bowl, beat eggs, half and half, tarragon, salt and pepper.
2. Melt butter or margarine in a medium skillet. Pour in egg mixture, tilting pan to cover bottom evenly.
3. Cook omelet until almost set; place under preheated broiler 30 seconds to cook top.
4. Garnish with tarragon, if desired. To serve, cut in half. Makes 2 serving.

Garlic & Anchovy Dip

Bagna Cauda

---

1 (2-oz.) can anchovies, drained
1/4 cup butter or margarine
1/4 cup olive oil
1 garlic clove, crushed

To serve:
French bread
Raw vegetables, such as zucchini, celery or carrot
 sticks; radishes; bell-pepper slices; and broccoli or
 cauliflower, broken into flowerets

This essentially peasant dish is best kept warm at the table in an earthenware pot.

1. Finely chop anchovies. Set aside.
2. Heat butter or margarine and olive oil in a small saucepan. Stir in garlic and chopped anchovies; simmer 10 minutes.
3. Pour into a small heatproof bowl; keep warm over a low flame. Serve warm with pieces of bread and raw vegetables for dipping. Makes 2 servings.

Spinach & Ricotta Tarts

Crostate di Spinaci e Ricotta

1/3 cup all-purpose flour
Pinch of salt
2 tablespoons butter or margarine
2 to 3 teaspoons water
Filling:
1/4 (10-oz.) pkg. thawed frozen chopped spinach
1/2 cup ricotta cheese or
   1 (3-oz.) pkg. Neufchâtel cheese, room temperature
2 teaspoons grated Parmesan cheese
2 pinches of ground nutmeg
1 egg, beaten
2 tablespoons half and half
Salt
Freshly ground pepper

The pastry recipe makes two tarts. If desired, double amounts and freeze extra tart shells for another use.

1. Preheat oven to 400F (205C). In a medium bowl, combine flour and salt. With a pastry blender or 2 knives, cut in butter or margarine until mixture resembles coarse crumbs.
2. Stir in water to make a firm dough. Knead lightly on a lightly floured surface.
3. Divide dough in half. Roll out each piece to a 6-inch circle. Use pastry to line 2 (4-inch) tart pans. Place pans on a baking sheet; prick pastry with a fork.
4. Bake in preheated oven 10 minutes.
5. Make filling while pastry bakes. In a medium bowl, combine all filling ingredients. Pour into baked pastry. Bake 20 to 25 minutes or until filling has just set and a knife inserted off center comes out clean. Serve warm or cold. Makes 2 servings.

Ham with Avocado

Prosciutto de Parma con Avocado

---

1 medium avocado
6 prosciutto slices, about 3 oz.

Dressing:
1 tablespoon olive oil
1 teaspoon lemon juice
1 garlic clove, crushed
2 teaspoons chopped fresh parsley
Salt
Freshly ground pepper

If avocados must stand before serving, dip slices in lemon juice to prevent browning.

1. Cut avocado in half; remove and discard pit. Peel; cut each half into 3 thick slices.
2. Wrap a ham slice around each avocado slice. Arrange ham-wrapped avocado slices in a serving dish.
3. To make dressing, place all dressing ingredients in a small container with a tight-fitting lid. Shake to combine.
4. To serve, pour dressing over ham and avocado. Makes 2 servings.

Variation
Ham with Figs (Prosciutto di Parma con Fichi): Cut 4 ripe figs into quarters. Arrange fig quarters and ham on serving plates. Omit dressing.

Avocados

To check if an avocado is ripe, hold it in your hand; squeeze gently. If it gives very slightly, the avocado is ripe. Avocados will continue to ripen at room temperature. Do not buy avocados that are very soft or have dark blemishes. When avocados are ripe, refrigerate to prevent overripening.

Eggs Stuffed with Peppers

Uova Farcite di Peperoni

---

2 hard-cooked eggs
1/2 small red bell pepper
Salt
1 tablespoon olive oil
1 teaspoon capers, finely chopped
2 teaspoons finely chopped fresh parsley
1 anchovy, finely chopped
1/2 teaspoon Dijon-style mustard
Freshly ground black pepper

To serve:
Shredded lettuce

---

1. Cut eggs in half; remove yolks. Sieve yolks into a small bowl; set aside. Reserve egg whites.
2. In a small saucepan, cook bell pepper in boiling salted water 5 minutes. Drain; pat dry with paper towels. Cut 8 thin strips from cooked pepper; set aside. Finely chop remaining pepper.
3. Add chopped pepper, olive oil, capers, parsley, anchovy, mustard, salt and pepper to sieved egg yolks. Stir to combine.
4. Spoon mixture into egg-white halves; crisscross 2 reserved pepper strips on each stuffed half.
5. Arrange lettuce on a serving plate. Place eggs on lettuce. Makes 2 servings.

Baked Peppers with Anchovies

Peperone con Alicia

---

1 medium green bell pepper
1 medium red bell pepper
2 garlic cloves, finely chopped
2 small tomatoes
4 anchovies
2 tablespoons olive oil

To serve:
Lemon slices

---

1. Preheat broiler. Place whole bell peppers under broiler, turning occasionally until charred. Cool slightly; remove skin with a small sharp knife. Cut each pepper in quarters; remove and discard seeds.
2. Preheat oven to 400F (205C). Grease a baking sheet. Place pepper quarters on greased baking sheet, with outsides down. Sprinkle with garlic. Slice each tomato into 4 slices; arrange tomatoes over garlic.
3. Halve each anchovy crosswise, then lengthwise. Arrange 2 anchovy pieces over each tomato slice. Drizzle with olive oil.
4. Bake in preheated oven 30 minutes or until bell peppers are crisp-tender. Serve hot or at room temperature. Garnish with lemon slices. Makes 2 servings.

Clockwise from left: Ham with Avocado, Baked Peppers with Anchovies, Eggs Stuffed with Peppers

Risotto Ring with Chicken-Liver Sauce

Anello di Risotto ai Fegatini

2 tablespoons butter or margarine
1 small onion, finely chopped
1 cup uncooked arborio or other short-grain rice
2 cups hot chicken stock
Salt
Freshly ground pepper

Chicken-Liver Sauce:
3 tablespoons olive oil
1 garlic clove, crushed
1 small onion, chopped
1 small green bell pepper, chopped
8 oz. chicken livers, coarsely chopped
1 teaspoon tomato paste
1/4 cup dry vermouth
2 tablespoons water
1 teaspoon chopped fresh sage or
  1/2 teaspoon rubbed sage
Salt
Freshly ground black pepper

To serve:
1 tablespoon grated Parmesan cheese
Fresh parsley

1. Melt butter or margarine in a medium saucepan. Add onion; sauté about 5 minutes or until soft. Stir in rice until all grains are coated with butter or margarine.
2. Add 1/4 of stock, salt and pepper; bring to a boil. Reduce heat. Simmer, uncovered, until stock is absorbed. Gradually stir in remaining stock; cook about 20 minutes or until rice is tender and liquid is absorbed.
3. Meanwhile, make sauce. To make sauce, heat olive oil in a medium skillet. Add garlic and onion; sauté about 5 minutes or until onion is soft.
4. Add bell pepper and chicken livers; sauté until livers are browned. Stir in tomato paste, vermouth, water and sage; season with salt and pepper. Simmer 10 minutes, stirring occasionally.
5. To serve, butter an 8-inch ring mold. Stir Parmesan cheese into hot cooked rice. Press into buttered ring mold. Loosen edges of rice. Place a serving plate over mold; invert. Remove mold.
6. Fill center of rice ring with hot sauce. Sprinkle chopped parsley over rice. Arrange parsley sprigs around rice ring. Makes 2 servings.

Risotto with Shrimp & Brandy

Risotto di Gamberoni

1-1/2 cups hot chicken stock
1/2 teaspoon saffron threads
6 tablespoons butter or margarine
1 small onion, chopped
1/2 (10-oz.) pkg. frozen cut green beans
1 cup uncooked arborio or other short-grain rice
1/2 cup white wine
1/4 (10-oz.) pkg. frozen green peas
2 teaspoons chopped chives
1 teaspoon chopped fresh dill or 1/2 teaspoon dried
  dill weed
Salt
Freshly ground pepper
2 to 3 teaspoons grated Parmesan cheese
1 small garlic clove, crushed
6 large, deveined, peeled, uncooked shrimp
2 tablespoons brandy

To garnish:
Dill sprigs

1. Pour hot stock over saffron threads; let stand about 30 minutes.
2. Melt 2 tablespoons butter or margarine in a medium saucepan. Add onion; sauté about 5 minutes or until soft. Add beans; cook 1 minute.
3. Stir in rice until all grains are coated with butter or margarine. Add 1/3 of stock and soaked saffron threads; bring to a boil. Reduce heat. Simmer, uncovered, until stock is absorbed.
4. Gradually stir in remaining 2/3 of stock with any remaining saffron threads and wine; cook about 20 minutes or until rice is tender and liquid is absorbed. Stir in peas 5 minutes before end of cooking time.
5. Stir chives, dill, salt, pepper, 2 tablespoons butter or margarine and Parmesan cheese into cooked rice. Keep rice warm while preparing shrimp.
6. Heat remaining 2 tablespoons butter or margarine in a medium skillet over medium heat. Add garlic. Cook 1 minute, stirring. Stir in shrimp. Season with salt and pepper; cook about 5 minutes or until shrimp turn pink. Add brandy; heat until hot. Ignite hot brandy; stir until flames go out.
7. Divide rice between 2 dishes, or serve on a single dish. Top with hot shrimp. Garnish with sprigs of dill. Makes 2 servings.

Left to right: Risotto with Shrimp & Brandy, Risotto Ring with Chicken-Liver Sauce

Zucchini Risotto

Risotto di Zucchini

---

2 tablespoons olive oil
1 small onion, sliced
1 celery stalk, chopped
1 small zucchini, thinly sliced
1 cup uncooked arborio or other short-grain rice
2 cups hot chicken stock
1/4 cup finely chopped cooked ham
Salt
Freshly ground pepper
2 tablespoons butter or margarine
1/3 cup grated Parmesan cheese (1 oz.)

---

1. Heat olive oil in a medium saucepan. Add onion and celery; sauté 5 minutes or until onion is soft. Add zucchini; sauté 1 minute.
2. Stir in rice until all grains are coated with oil. Add 1/4 of hot stock; bring to a boil. Reduce heat. Simmer, uncovered, until stock is absorbed. Gradually stir in remaining stock; cook about 20 minutes or until rice is tender and liquid is absorbed.
3. Stir in ham, salt and pepper; cook until hot. Remove from heat; quickly stir in butter or margarine and cheese. Spoon into a warm serving dish. Serve hot as a side dish or a starter. Makes 2 servings.

Pizza Turnovers

Calzone

---

1 teaspoon active dry yeast
1/2 teaspoon sugar
1/4 cup warm water (110F, 45C)
3/4 cup plus 2 tablespoons all-purpose flour
1/2 teaspoon salt
1 tablespoon olive oil
Vegetable oil

Filling:
2 thin ham slices
4 mozzarella-cheese slices (2 oz.)
4 fresh marjoram sprigs or
   1 teaspoon dried leaf marjoram
Salt
Freshly ground pepper
Olive oil

If made ahead, keep warm in a 325F (165C) oven up to 30 minutes. Serve one per person as a starter or two per person as a main dish.

1. In a small bowl, dissolve yeast and sugar in water. Let stand 5 to 10 minutes or until foamy.
2. In a small bowl, combine flour and salt. Stir in olive oil and yeast mixture to make a soft dough. Knead on a lightly floured surface about 5 minutes.
3. Wash and grease bowl. Place dough in clean bowl; turn to coat. Cover with a damp towel. Let rise in a warm place, free from drafts, 40 minutes or until doubled in bulk.
4. Punch down dough. Divide dough into 4 pieces. On a lightly floured surface, roll out each piece into a 5-inch circle. Cut ham slices in half. Place a cheese slice on each circle. Top cheese with a half slice of ham, a sprig of marjoram or 1/4 teaspoon dried marjoram, salt, pepper and a drizzle of olive oil. Fold dough in half; press edges to seal.
5. Meanwhile, heat oil to 350F (175C) or until a 1-inch bread cube turns golden brown in 65 seconds. Fry turnovers, 2 at a time, 4 to 5 minutes or until golden brown.
6. Drain on paper towels; serve warm in a folded napkin. As a main course, serve with Beet & Radish Salad, page 67. Makes 2 main-dish servings or 4 appetizer servings.

1/On a lightly floured surface, knead dough 5 minutes.

2/Divide dough into 4 pieces. Roll out each piece to a 5-inch circle.

3/Place cheese, ham and herbs on each circle.

4/Fold dough in half; press edges to seal.

Left to right: Pine-Nut Pizza, Pizza Turnovers

Pine-Nut Pizzas

Pinocchiate

---

1 recipe yeast dough from Pizza Turnovers, opposite
3 tablespoons olive oil
2 medium onions, thinly sliced
1 small red bell pepper, sliced
Salt
Freshly ground black pepper
4 oz. Bel Paese cheese
1/4 cup sliced pimento-stuffed green olives
1/4 cup pine nuts
2 teaspoons grated Parmesan cheese
1 teaspoon dried leaf basil

---

1. Prepare dough as directed opposite through step 3.
2. Meanwhile, heat olive oil in a medium skillet. Add onions; sauté 5 minutes. Add bell pepper, salt and black pepper; sauté 5 minutes or until peppers are soft. Cool to room temperature.
3. Preheat oven to 400F (205C). Grease a large baking sheet. Punch down dough. Divide dough in half. On a lightly floured surface, roll out each half to an 8-inch circle. Place circles on greased baking sheet.
4. Spread onion mixture evenly over each circle. Thinly slice Bel Paese cheese; arrange over onion mixture. Sprinkle cheese with olives and pine nuts; top with Parmesan cheese. Sprinkle with basil. Pizza can be refrigerated up to 8 hours or frozen up to 1 month.
5. Bake in preheated oven 35 minutes or until cheese melts and crust is golden brown. If cooking from frozen, add 10 minutes to baking time. Serve hot. Makes 2 servings.

Heart-Shaped Pizza

Pizza di Cuore

---

1 recipe yeast dough from Pizza Turnovers, page 22
1 (8-oz.) can tomatoes
2 teaspoons dried leaf oregano
1 garlic clove, crushed
1 teaspoon sugar
Salt
Freshly ground pepper
4 oz. mozzarella cheese
5 canned artichoke hearts, drained, halved
10 anchovy fillets
1 tablespoon chopped fresh parsley

---

1. Prepare dough as directed on page 22 through step 3.
2. In a medium saucepan, combine tomatoes with their liquid, 1 teaspoon oregano, garlic, sugar, salt and pepper. Bring to a boil. Reduce heat. Simmer about 10 minutes or until thickened. Cool to room temperature.
3. Preheat oven to 400F (205C). Grease a baking sheet. Punch down dough. On a lightly floured surface, roll out dough to a 10-inch circle. Make a 3-inch cut from edge toward center; tuck under cut edges to form a heart shape. Shape opposite side into a point.
4. Place dough on greased baking sheet. Spread cooled tomato sauce evenly over top. Cut mozzarella cheese into 10 slices; place slices around edge of pizza. Place artichoke hearts between cheese slices. Cut each anchovy fillet in half lengthwise. Crisscross 2 strips on each cheese slice. Sprinkle remaining teaspoon of oregano and parsley over top.
5. Bake in preheated oven 35 minutes or until cheese melts and crust is golden brown. Serve hot. Makes 2 servings.

Four Seasons' Pizza

Pizza Quatro Stagioni

---

1 recipe yeast dough from Pizza Turnovers, page 22
Tomato Sauce:
1 (8-oz.) can tomatoes
1 teaspoon dried leaf oregano
1 teaspoon sugar
1 tablespoon tomato paste
Salt
Freshly ground pepper
Toppings:
4 oz. mozzarella cheese, coarsely chopped
3/4 cup sliced mushrooms (about 2 oz.)
1/4 cup chopped cooked ham
1 (3-1/2-oz.) can water-pack tuna, drained, flaked
1 small green or red bell pepper, cut into thin strips
8 ripe olives

---

1. Prepare dough as directed on page 22 through step 3.
2. To make sauce, in a medium saucepan, combine tomatoes with their liquid, oregano, sugar, tomato paste, salt and pepper. Bring to a boil. Reduce heat. Simmer about 10 minutes or until thickened. Cool to room temperature.
3. Preheat oven to 400F (205C). Grease a baking sheet. Punch down dough. Divide dough into 2 pieces, making 1 piece 2/3 of dough. Divide small piece of dough into 2 pieces; set aside.
4. On a lightly floured surface, roll out large piece of dough into a 9-inch circle. Place on greased baking sheet.
5. Spread cooled tomato sauce over dough; sprinkle with mozzarella cheese. Shape each small piece of dough into a 9-inch-long strip. Crisscross strips across dough to divide it into 4 equal sections; seal ends.
6. Fill 1 section with mushrooms; fill opposite section with ham. Fill 1 remaining section with tuna; fill last section with bell pepper. Arrange olives evenly around edge of pizza.
7. Bake in preheated oven 35 minutes or until cheese melts and crust is golden brown. Serve hot. Makes 2 servings.

Tomato Risotto

Risotto alla Pomodoro

2 tablespoons olive oil
1 medium onion, finely chopped
1 cup uncooked arborio or other short-grain rice
Tomato Sauce from Four Seasons' Pizza, opposite
1-1/2 cups hot chicken stock
Salt
Freshly ground pepper

1. Heat oil in a medium saucepan. Add onion; sauté about 5 minutes or until soft. Stir in rice until all grains are coated with oil.

2. Add Tomato Sauce, 1/4 of stock, salt and pepper. Bring to a boil. Reduce heat. Simmer, uncovered, until stock is absorbed. Gradually stir in remaining stock; cook about 20 minutes or until rice is tender and all liquid is absorbed.

3. Serve hot. Makes 2 servings.

Variation
Mozzarella & Basil Risotto (Risotto alla Romana) Omit Tomato Sauce; increase stock to 2 cups. Just before serving, stir in 2 teaspoons chopped fresh basil and 4 ounces cubed mozzarella cheese. Stir gently until cheese melts.

Left to right: Tossed salad, Heart-Shaped Pizza

Rice Pilaf with Mushrooms

Riso ai Funghi

1/2 teaspoon saffron threads
1-1/2 cups hot chicken stock
3 tablespoons olive oil
2 shallots, finely chopped
3/4 cup uncooked arborio or other short-grain rice
1 bay leaf
Salt
Freshly ground pepper
1 garlic clove, crushed
4 oz. cèpe mushrooms, sliced
2 tablespoons white wine

To garnish:
2 teaspoons chopped chives

See page 8 for information about cèpe mushrooms.

1. Place saffron in a medium bowl; pour hot stock over saffron. Let stand about 30 minutes.
2. Heat 2 tablespoons olive oil in a medium saucepan. Add shallots; sauté 5 minutes or until soft.
3. Stir in rice until all grains are coated with oil. Add stock with soaked saffron threads, bay leaf, salt and pepper. Bring to a boil. Reduce heat. Cover; simmer 30 minutes or until rice is tender and stock is absorbed.
4. Meanwhile, heat remaining 1 tablespoon olive oil in a small saucepan. Add garlic; sauté 1 minute. Stir in mushrooms. Add wine, salt and pepper; simmer 15 to 20 minutes or until mushrooms are tender.
5. Spoon rice into a warm serving dish; pour mushrooms over top. Sprinkle with chives. Serve as a side dish or starter. Makes 2 servings.

Left to right: Rice Pilaf with Mushrooms, Rice Croquettes with Mozzarella & Ham

Veal & Bacon Lasagna

Lasagne

Veal & Bacon Sauce:
2 tablespoons olive oil
1 small onion, chopped
1 garlic clove, crushed
2 bacon slices, diced
12 oz. ground veal
2 teaspoons chopped fresh sage or 1 teaspoon dried
  leaf sage
1 tomato, peeled, chopped
1/2 cup white wine
Salt
Freshly ground pepper

Bechamel Sauce:
2 tablespoons butter or margarine
1/4 cup all-purpose flour
1 cup milk
1/2 cup half and half
Pinch of ground nutmeg
Salt
Freshly ground pepper
1/3 cup grated Parmesan cheese (1 oz.)
6 lasagna noodles, cooked

---

1. Heat olive oil in a medium saucepan. Add onion, garlic and bacon; sauté 5 minutes or until onion is soft. Add veal; stir until veal is no longer pink.
2. Stir in sage, tomato, wine, salt and pepper. Bring to a boil. Reduce heat. Simmer 20 minutes or until thickened. Set aside.
3. Preheat oven to 400F (205C). Grease a 9'' x 5'' loaf dish. To make sauce, melt butter or margarine in a medium saucepan. Stir in flour; cook 1 minute, stirring. Gradually stir in milk; cook until thickened, stirring. Stir in half and half and nutmeg. Season with salt and pepper; cook 2 minutes, stirring.
4. Spread a little bechamel sauce in bottom of greased dish. Sprinkle with 1 tablespoon cheese.
5. Arrange 2 noodles over cheese; do not overlap pieces. Spread 1/3 of remaining bechamel sauce evenly over noodles. Sprinkle with 1 tablespoon cheese. Spoon 1/3 of meat sauce over cheese.
6. Repeat layers twice more, beginning with 2 noodles and ending with meat sauce and remaining cheese. Lasagna can be covered and refrigerated up to 24 hours.
7. Bake in preheated oven 35 minutes or until mixture is bubbling. Makes 2 servings.

Rice Croquettes with Mozzarella & Ham

Suppli

---

2 tablespoons olive oil
1 small onion, finely chopped
1 cup uncooked arborio or other short-grain rice
2 cups hot chicken stock
Salt
Freshly ground pepper
2 oz. mozzarella cheese, cut into 6 slices
2 oz. prosciutto, cut into 6 slices
1 cup fresh white-bread crumbs
2 teaspoons grated Parmesan cheese
2 teaspoons chopped fresh parsley
Vegetable oil

---

1. Heat olive oil in a medium saucepan. Add onion; sauté 5 minutes or until soft. Stir in rice until all grains are coated with oil.
2. Add 1/4 of hot stock; bring to a boil. Reduce heat. Simmer, uncovered, until stock is absorbed. Gradually stir in remaining stock; cook about 20 minutes or until rice is tender and liquid is absorbed. Season with salt and pepper. Cool, cover and refrigerate until rice is cold.
3. Divide rice into 6 equal portions. Divide each portion in half; flatten each half with your hands to form cakes about 3 inches across.
4. Lay a mozzarella-cheese slice and a ham slice on 1 rice cake; trim cheese and ham to fit, if necessary. Top with another rice cake; press edges to seal.
5. Repeat with remaining rice, mozzarella cheese and ham. In a shallow bowl, combine bread crumbs, Parmesan cheese and parsley. Coat each croquette with bread-crumb mixture, pressing mixture into rice. Croquettes can be covered and refrigerated up to 24 hours.
6. To cook, heat about 1 inch of oil in a large skillet over medium heat. Add croquettes; fry about 4 minutes on each side or until golden brown and crisp.
7. Drain on paper towels; serve hot. Makes 2 servings of 3 croquettes each.

Noodles with Chicken & Tomatoes

Fettucine con Pollo

1 tablespoon olive oil
1 boneless chicken-breast half, skinned, chopped
1 small onion, chopped
1 celery stalk, chopped
1 small carrot, diced
1 teaspoon dried leaf oregano
1/4 cup red wine
1 (8-oz.) can tomatoes
Salt
Freshly ground pepper
6 oz. fettucine or tagliatelle

To garnish:
Celery leaves

1. Heat olive oil in a medium saucepan. Add chicken; sauté until lightly browned. Add onion, celery and carrot; cook 5 minutes or until vegetables are soft, stirring occasionally.
2. Stir in oregano, wine, tomatoes, salt and pepper. Bring to a boil. Reduce heat. Cover; simmer 10 minutes.
3. Meanwhile, cook noodles in a large pot of boiling salted water 8 minutes or until just tender to the bite or al dente.
4. Drain well; stir drained noodles into chicken sauce. Spoon into a warm serving dish; garnish with celery leaves. Makes 2 servings.

Seafood Spaghetti

Spaghetti alla Marinara

6 oz. spaghetti
2 tablespoons olive oil
2 garlic cloves, crushed
8 oz. mussels in shells
4 oz. deveined, peeled, uncooked shrimp
1/4 cup white wine
Salt
Freshly ground black pepper
1/2 cup whipping cream
Pinch of red (cayenne) pepper
1 tablespoon chopped fresh parsley

To garnish:
4 unpeeled cooked shrimp
1 lemon slice, quartered

1. Scrub mussels; remove beards. Discard any mussels that remain open. Place cleaned mussels in a heavy pan over medium heat; cover tightly. Cook 3 to 5 minutes or until shells open. Remove cooked mussels with a slotted spoon; discard cooking liquid. Remove cooked mussels from shells; discard shells, reserving mussels for sauce.
2. Cook spaghetti in a large pot of boiling salted water 8 to 10 minutes or until just tender to the bite or al dente.
3. Meanwhile, heat 1 tablespoon olive oil in a medium saucepan. Add garlic; sauté 1 minute. Add mussels, shrimp, wine, salt and black pepper. Cook 3 minutes.
4. Stir in cream and red pepper; heat until hot.
5. Drain spaghetti; stir in remaining 1 tablespoon olive oil and parsley. Divide spaghetti between 2 warm bowls; spoon seafood sauce over spaghetti. Garnish with shrimp and lemon. Makes 2 servings.

Pasta Bows in Walnut-Cheese Sauce

Farfalle al Mascarpone e Noce

6 oz. pasta bows

Walnut-Cheese Sauce:
1/2 (8-oz.) pkg. Neufchâtel cheese
1/2 cup half and half
1 tablespoon grated Parmesan cheese
Salt
Freshly ground pepper
1 to 2 tablespoons milk
1 tablespoon olive oil
1 teaspoon lemon juice

To garnish:
1/4 cup coarsely chopped walnuts
2 teaspoons chopped chives

1. Cook pasta bows in a large pot of boiling salted water 6 to 8 minutes or until just tender to the bite or al dente. Meanwhile make sauce.
2. To make sauce, heat Neufchâtel cheese in a medium saucepan over low heat until it forms a thick sauce. Stir in half and half, Parmesan cheese, salt and pepper. Cook, stirring, until smooth and creamy. If mixture is too thick, stir in milk.
3. Drain pasta; toss with olive oil and lemon juice. Divide pasta between 2 dishes. Spoon sauce over pasta. Garnish with walnuts and chives. Makes 2 servings.

Top to bottom: Noodles with Chicken & Tomatoes, Pasta Bows in Walnut-Cheese Sauce, Seafood Spaghetti

Left to right: Macaroni with Sausage & Tomato Sauce, Ricotta &
Spinach Cannelloni, Wine punch

Macaroni with Sausage & Tomato Sauce

Macaroni alla Romagnola

8 oz. Italian sausage
1 tablespoon olive oil
1 garlic clove, crushed
1 small onion, coarsely chopped
1 small red bell pepper, finely chopped
3 medium tomatoes, peeled, chopped
1 tablespoon tomato paste
3 tablespoons Marsala or sherry
1 teaspoon dried leaf oregano
Salt
Freshly ground pepper
4 oz. macaroni
1 tablespoon butter or margarine

Many delicatessens and supermarkets sell Italian sausages. To serve as a starter, omit sausage; simply sprinkle tomato sauce with some grated Parmesan cheese.

1. Skin sausage; shape into 4 or 5 balls. Heat olive oil in a medium saucepan. Add garlic and onion; sauté 5 minutes or until onion is soft.
2. Add skinned sausage pieces to pan; cook until evenly browned. Drain off excess fat. Add bell pepper, tomatoes, tomato paste, Marsala or sherry, oregano, salt and pepper. Simmer 15 minutes or until thickened.
3. Meanwhile, cook macaroni in a large pot of boiling salted water 8 to 10 minutes or until just tender to the bite or al dente. Drain well; stir in butter or margarine.
4. Stir buttered macaroni into tomato sauce. Spoon into a warm serving dish or 2 individual dishes. Makes 2 servings.

Ricotta & Spinach Cannelloni

Cannelloni Piacentini

8 oz. fresh spinach or
   1/2 (10-oz.) pkg. thawed frozen chopped spinach
1/2 cup ricotta cheese, drained
1 tablespoon grated Parmesan cheese
2 pinches of ground nutmeg
1 egg yolk
1 tablespoon chopped fresh mixed herbs or
   1 teaspoon dried leaf herbs (marjoram, chives,
   parsley or chervil)
Salt
Freshly ground pepper
8 cooked cannelloni noodles
2 tablespoons grated Parmesan cheese

Tomato Sauce:
4 medium tomatoes, peeled, chopped
1 small onion, chopped
1 celery stalk, chopped
1 tablespoon tomato paste
1/2 teaspoon sugar
Freshly ground pepper

1. Grease a shallow casserole large enough to hold cannelloni in 1 layer. If using fresh spinach, wash, remove large stems and chop. Place chopped spinach in a medium saucepan with only water that clings to leaves. Cover; cook 5 to 7 minutes, shaking pan occasionally, or until spinach is tender. Drain well. Drain frozen spinach, if using.
2. Place drained spinach in a bowl. Stir in ricotta cheese, Parmesan cheese, nutmeg, egg yolk, herbs, salt and pepper.
3. Using a small spoon, carefully fill cannelloni tubes with spinach mixture. Place filled cannelloni in greased casserole.
4. To make sauce, combine all sauce ingredients in a medium saucepan. Bring to a boil. Reduce heat. Simmer 20 minutes or until vegetables are soft.
5. Preheat oven to 350F (175C). Press tomato sauce through a sieve or puree in a blender until almost smooth. Pour tomato sauce evenly over filled cannelloni, covering completely. Sprinkle with Parmesan cheese.
6. Bake in preheated oven 35 to 40 minutes or until heated through and sauce is bubbling. Makes 2 servings.

Green Noodles with Cream, Ham & Mushrooms

Tagliatelle Verdi alla Ghiotta

3 tablespoons butter or margarine
2 shallots or small onions, finely chopped
1/2 cup diced cooked ham
1-1/2 cups sliced mushrooms (about 4 oz.)
1/2 cup whipping cream
1 tablespoon chopped fresh parsley
1 tablespoon grated Parmesan cheese
Salt
Freshly ground pepper
6 oz. spinach tagliatelle

This dish is very quick to prepare. Measure and prepare all ingredients in advance for a fast final assembly. If possible, use fresh or frozen pasta for this dish.

1. Melt 2 tablespoons butter or margarine in a medium skillet. Add shallots or onions; sauté 5 minutes or until soft. Add ham and mushrooms; cook 2 minutes.
2. Stir in cream, parsley, 2 teaspoons Parmesan cheese, salt and pepper. Reduce heat; simmer 5 minutes.
3. Meanwhile, cook noodles in a large pot of boiling salted water 7 to 8 minutes or until just tender to the bite or al dente. Drain well; stir in remaining 1 tablespoon butter or margarine and 1 teaspoon Parmesan cheese.
4. Place noodles in a warmed serving dish; make a well in center. Pour in sauce; serve at once. Makes 2 servings.

Serving Pasta

There are several delicious ways to make pasta taste extra special. Cook it as described on page 9. Drain well; just before serving, stir in any one of following:

1. Two tablespoons butter or margarine, one teaspoon chopped fresh parsley, marjoram or tarragon and one tablespoon lemon juice;
2. Two tablespoons butter or margarine and one tablespoon pine nuts;
3. One tablespoon Basil Sauce (Pesto,) page 13;
4. One tablespoon grated Parmesan cheese and two tablespoons butter or margarine; or
5. One-half recipe Tomato Sauce from Four Seasons' Pizza, page 24.

Always use a warm serving dish, otherwise pasta will cool quickly and become less appetizing.

Marinated Shrimp Kabobs

Scampi agli Stecchi

---

8 oz. medium, deveined, peeled, uncooked shrimp

Marinade:
2 garlic cloves, crushed
3 tablespoons olive oil
2 tablespoons chopped fresh parsley
2 teaspoons lemon juice
1 tablespoon dry white bread crumbs
Salt
Freshly ground pepper
Bay leaves

---

1. Rinse shrimp; pat dry with paper towels.
2. In a small bowl, combine garlic, olive oil, parsley, lemon juice, bread crumbs, salt and pepper. Stir in shrimp until coated. Cover and refrigerate at least 1 hour or up to 8 hours.
3. Preheat broiler. Thread marinated shrimp onto 4 skewers, using 3 or 4 bay leaves for each skewer. Place skewers on an ungreased baking sheet.
4. Cook 4 to 6 inches from heat, turning occasionally, until coating is crisp and shrimp are pink.
5. Serve hot with Rice Pilaf with Mushrooms, page 26, and a tossed salad or Raddicchio Salad, page 65.
6. Serve with a dry white wine or a light red wine. Makes 2 servings.

Marinating Fish

Marinating ready-to-cook whole fish such as flounder, sole or trout, adds a special flavor and succulence. To make a marinade, in a small bowl, combine 1/4 cup olive oil; 1 tablespoon lemon juice; 2 teaspoons chopped fresh herbs or 1 teaspoon dried leaf herbs, such as rosemary, chives, or mint; salt and freshly ground pepper. Using a sharp knife, make 3 shallow diagonal cuts across each side of the fish. Place slashed fish in a shallow dish. Pour marinade over fish. Cover and refrigerate at least 2 hours or up to 12 hours. The longer marinating time will give a better flavor. Broil or grill fish, basting occasionally with marinade. Cook flounder or sole 8 to 10 minutes and trout 12 to 15 minutes, depending on thickness and size.

Salmon with Caper & Parsley Sauce

Salmone con Salsa Piccante

---

2 (4- to 6-oz.) salmon steaks
Salt
Freshly ground pepper

Poaching Liquid:
1/2 cup dry white wine
1 bay leaf
3 parsley sprigs
1 shallot or small onion, chopped
Celery leaves

Caper & Parsley Sauce:
2 tablespoons butter or margarine
1 garlic clove, crushed
1 tablespoon capers, drained, chopped
2 tablespoons chopped fresh parsley
Salt
Freshly ground pepper

To garnish:
Celery leaves

---

1. Wipe fish with paper towels. Sprinkle both sides with salt and pepper.
2. Place all poaching ingredients in a shallow pan large enough to hold fish in a single layer; bring liquid to a simmer. Add fish; cover. Simmer about 12 minutes or until fish turns from translucent to opaque and just begins to flake when pierced with a fork in thickest part.
3. Remove poached fish from liquid; place on a warm serving plate. Keep warm while preparing sauce. To make sauce, strain poaching liquid; reserve 1/4 cup.
4. Melt butter or butter in a small saucepan. Add garlic, capers and parsley; cook 1 minute, stirring. Add salt, pepper and reserved poaching liquid.
5. Bring to a boil; pour over fish. Garnish with celery leaves.
6. Serve with a light dry white wine. Makes 2 servings.

Top to bottom: Green salad, Marinated Shrimp Kabobs, Salmon with Caper & Parsley Sauce

Halibut with Raisins & Olives

Pesce con Prunite è Oliva

---

2 (4- to 6-oz.) halibut steaks
1/4 cup all-purpose flour
Salt
Freshly ground pepper
2 tablespoons olive oil
1 garlic clove, crushed
1 small onion, chopped
1 celery stalk, chopped
1/4 cup raisins
6 pitted green olives
1/4 cup white wine
Salt
Freshly ground pepper

To garnish:
Celery leaves

---

1. Wipe fish with paper towels. In a shallow bowl, combine flour, salt and pepper. Coat fish in seasoned flour.
2. Heat olive oil in a medium skillet. Add floured fish; sauté 10 to 12 minutes or until golden brown and fish just begins to flake when pierced with a fork in thickest part, turning once.
3. With a wide spatula, carefully remove sautéed fish from skillet. Place on a warm serving plate. Keep warm.
4. Add garlic, onion and celery to skillet; sauté about 5 minutes or until onion is soft. Stir in raisins, olives, wine, salt and pepper. Simmer 5 minutes.
5. Pour sauce over fish; garnish with celery leaves. Serve with sautéed or steamed potatoes.
6. Serve with a dry white wine. Makes 2 servings.

Left to right: Halibut with Raisins & Olives, Sea Bass with Mint

Baked Trout

Trota in Cartoccio

---

2 (12-oz.) trout, cleaned, page 39
Salt
Freshly ground pepper
2 tablespoons olive oil
2 garlic cloves, crushed
1 medium onion. chopped
1 celery stalk, chopped
4 rosemary sprigs
2 tablespoons white wine

To garnish:
Rosemary sprigs

---

1. Preheat oven to 350F (175C). Wipe fish with paper towels. Sprinkle inside and out with salt and pepper.
2. Heat olive oil in a large skillet. Add garlic, onion and celery; sauté 5 minutes or onion is until soft. Add salt, pepper, 2 rosemary sprigs and wine; cook 5 minutes.
3. Cut 2 double sheets of parchment paper each łarge enough to enclose 1 fish. Brush paper with oil. Divide sautéed vegetables between oiled paper; place a fish on each vegetable portion. Place 2 remaining rosemary sprigs on fish. Wrap fish as shown below; place on a baking sheet.
4. Bake in preheated oven 20 minutes or until fish turns from translucent to opaque and just begins to flake when pierced with a fork in thickest part.
5. Remove fish from paper; place on 2 plates. Garnish with rosemary sprigs.
6. Serve with a fruity dry white wine. Makes 2 servings.

Variation
Substitute mullet, mackerel or salmon steaks for trout.

Sea Bass with Mint

Spigole alla Menta

---

1 (1-1/2-lb.) sea bass, cleaned, page 39
Salt
Freshly ground pepper
About 2 cups mint leaves
2 tablespoons butter or margarine, room temperature
1 cup fresh bread crumbs
2 tablespoons lemon juice
Olive oil
1/2 cup dry white wine

To serve:
Mint sprigs
3 or 4 lemon slices, quartered

---

1. Preheat oven to 350F (175C). Wipe fish with paper towels. Sprinkle inside and out with salt and pepper.
2. Chop 2 tablespoons mint leaves; reserve remaining leaves. In a medium bowl, combine chopped mint, butter or margarine, bread crumbs, lemon juice, salt and pepper. Stuff mixture into fish cavity.
3. Place fish in a baking dish; brush with olive oil. Arrange remaining mint leaves, overlapping, to cover fish. Pour wine around fish; cover with foil.
4. Bake in preheated oven 40 to 45 minutes or until fish turns from translucent to opaque and just begins to flake when pierced with a fork in thickest part. Arrange mint sprigs along sides of a platter. Place fish in center of mint. Arrange lemon-slice quarters down center of fish. Serve with Asparagus with Egg, page 56.
5. Serve with a dry white wine. Makes 2 servings.

1/Brush sheets of parchment paper with oil.

2/Divide sautéed vegetables between oiled paper. Place a fish on each vegetable portion.

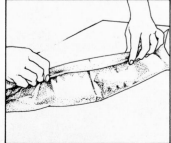

3/Fold paper over fish; close with a double fold.

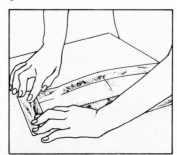

4/Double fold ends of paper to seal.

Seafood Casserole

Zuppa di Pesce

2 tablespoons olive oil
1 garlic clove, crushed
1 medium onion, chopped
1 small red bell pepper, chopped
12 oz. mixed uncooked seafood (fish pieces, peeled shrimp or scallops)
2 medium tomatoes, peeled, sliced
1/2 cup white wine
2 oz. fresh whole mushrooms
Salt
Freshly ground black pepper

To serve:
Toasted French bread

1. Heat olive oil in a medium saucepan. Add garlic and onion; sauté 5 minutes or until onion is soft.
2. Add bell pepper; sauté 2 minutes. Add seafood; stir to combine.
3. Add tomatoes, wine, mushrooms, salt and black pepper. Bring to a boil. Reduce heat. Simmer 10 minutes or until seafood turns from translucent to opaque.
4. Spoon into a warm serving dish. Serve with French bread and a green salad.
5. Serve a light dry white wine or a light red wine. Makes 2 servings.

Squid in Red Wine

Calamari in Umido

8 oz. squid, ready to cook
2 tablespoons lemon juice
3 tablespoons olive oil
1 large onion, sliced, separated into rings
2 garlic cloves, crushed
2 medium tomatoes, peeled, chopped
Sprig each of thyme and marjoram
1 cup red wine
1 tablespoon tomato paste
Salt
Freshly ground pepper

To garnish:
Thyme sprigs or marjoram sprigs
Lemon wedges

Ask your fish market to prepare the squid, or buy frozen squid which is already prepared. Squid lends itself well to a rich sauce such as this one.

1. Preheat oven to 325F (165C). Slice squid thinly into rings. In a medium bowl, combine sliced squid and lemon juice; marinate 1 hour.
2. Heat olive oil in a flameproof casserole. Add onion and garlic; sauté 5 minutes or until onion is soft. Add marinated squid; cook 2 minutes.
3. Stir in tomatoes, herbs, wine, tomato paste, salt and pepper. Bring to a boil; cover casserole.
4. Bake in preheated oven 1-1/4 hours or until squid is tender. Garnish with thyme or marjoram sprigs and lemon wedges. Serve with Polenta with Cheese, page 59, or Zucchini Risotto, page 22.
5. Serve with a robust red wine. Makes 2 servings.

Left to right: Seafood Casserole, Squid in Red Wine, Shrimp Fritters with Green Mayonnaise

Shrimp Fritters with Green Mayonnaise

Frittura di Scampi alla Maionese Verde

---

8 large, deveined, peeled, uncooked shrimp
1 tablespoon lemon juice
Salt
Freshly ground pepper

Green Mayonnaise:
1/2 cup mayonnaise
3 tablespoons chopped fresh parsley
2 teaspoons chopped fresh basil
1 tablespoon pine nuts, finely chopped
1 tablespoon pistachios, chopped
1 garlic clove, if desired, crushed
Salt
Freshly ground pepper

Batter:
7 tablespoons all-purpose flour
Salt

Freshly ground pepper
2 tablespoons olive oil
1/4 cup water
1 egg white
Vegetable oil

To serve:
Cucumber slices
Endive leaves

---

1. In a medium bowl, combine shrimp, lemon juice, salt and pepper; cover and refrigerate up to 24 hours.
2. In a small bowl, combine all ingredients for mayonnaise; cover and refrigerate until served or up to 24 hours.
3. To make batter, in a medium bowl, blend flour, salt and pepper. Stir in olive oil and water to make a smooth batter.
4. In a small bowl, beat egg white until soft peaks form. Fold beaten egg white into batter.
5. Heat oil to 350F (175C) or until a 1-inch bread cube turns golden brown in 65 seconds. Pat shrimp dry with paper towels. Dip shrimp in batter; deep-fry about 5 minutes or until batter is golden and shrimp are pink. Drain fried shrimp on paper towels.
6. To serve, place 4 or 5 cucumber slices on each plate; top with 1/2 of mayonnaise. Add 4 fried shrimp to each plate. Garnish with endive.
7. Serve with a dry white wine. Makes 2 servings.

Fish with Tomatoes & Anchovies

Triglie alla Griglia

---

3 tablespoons olive oil
1 garlic clove, crushed
1 (8-oz.) can tomatoes
3 anchovy fillets, chopped
2 tablespoons chopped fresh parsley
Pinch of sugar
Freshly ground pepper
2 redfish (about 1 lb. each) cleaned, below
Salt

To garnish:
2 anchovy fillets, halved lengthwise
Cilantro sprigs

---

1. Heat 2 tablespoons olive oil in a small saucepan. Add garlic; sauté until lightly browned. Stir in tomatoes with their liquid, anchovies, parsley, sugar and pepper. Bring to a boil. Reduce heat. Simmer 20 minutes or until thickened.
2. Meanwhile preheat broiler and cook fish. To cook fish, wipe dry with paper towels. Sprinkle fish inside and out with salt and pepper. Brush skin with remaining 1 tablespoon olive oil. Make 2 shallow diagonal cuts in each side of fish. Place fish on a broiler-pan rack.
3. Cook fish about 4 to 6 inches from preheated broiler 7 minutes per side or until fish turns from translucent to opaque and just begins to flake when pierced with a fork in thickest part. Place on a warm serving dish; pour some sauce over fish. Serve remaining sauce separately. Garnish with strips of anchovy and cilantro. Serve with Deep-Fried Artichoke Hearts, page 61.
4. Serve with a light red wine. Makes 2 servings.

Cleaning Fish

To clean a whole fish, hold fish firmly by tail with paper towels. To remove scales, with a dull knife blade or fish scaler, scrape from tail to head in short firm strokes. Do this in sink or on newspaper to catch scales; cut off fins. Next, cut down belly from head to anal opening, being careful not to pierce viscera; remove viscera. Run point of knife down both sides of backbone to puncture blood vessels. Remove head, if desired. Wash fish thoroughly under cold running water; pat dry with paper towels.

Fish with Tomatoes & Anchovies

Left to right: Cold Orange-Marinated Trout, Venetian-Style Sole, Stuffed Sardines

Cold Orange-Marinated Trout

Trota Marinata all'Arancia

2 (12-oz.) trout, cleaned, page 39
1/4 cup all-purpose flour
Salt
Freshly ground pepper
1/4 cup olive oil

Marinade:
2 medium oranges, halved
1 medium lemon, halved
1 small onion, finely chopped
1/2 cup dry white wine
2 bay leaves
Salt
Freshly ground pepper

To garnish:
1-1/2 orange slices, quartered

1. Wipe fish with paper towels. In a shallow bowl, combine flour, salt and pepper. Coat fish with seasoned flour.
2. Heat 3 tablespoons olive oil in a large skillet. Add floured fish; cook 12 minutes or until fish turns from translucent to opaque and just begins to flake when pierced with a fork at thickest part, turning once. Drain on paper towels. Place in a serving dish.
3. To make marinade, cut colored peel from an orange half and a lemon half; do not include any white pith. Cut peel into thin julienne strips. Place orange peel and lemon peel in a medium bowl; pour boiling water over peel. Let stand 20 minutes. Meanwhile, squeeze juice from all orange and lemon halves.
4. Heat remaining 1 tablespoon olive oil in a small saucepan. Add onion; sauté 5 minutes or until soft. Drain orange and lemon peel, discarding liquid. Add drained peel, orange juice, lemon juice, wine, bay leaves, salt and pepper to onion.
5. Pour onion mixture over fish. Cover and refrigerate at least 6 hours or overnight.
6. Garnish fish with orange slices. Serve chilled.
7. Serve with a fruity dry white wine. Makes 2 servings.

1. Wipe fish with paper towels. Using a sharp knife, make 2 or 3 diagonal cuts in each side of fish.
2. To make Savory Butter, in a small bowl, blend all ingredients. Spread 1/4 of mixture over 1 side of fish; reserve remaining butter mixture. Place fish, buttered-side up, in a broiler pan.
3. Preheat broiler. To make sauce, melt butter or margarine in a small saucepan. Add shallot; sauté about 5 minutes or until soft. Stir in wine, salt and pepper; cook 2 minutes. Keep warm while cooking fish.
4. Cook fish about 4 to 6 inches from preheated broiler 3 or 4 minutes. Turn fish; spread with remaining butter mixture. Cook 3 minutes or until fish turns from translucent to opaque and just begins to flake when pierced with a fork at thickest part.
5. Place fish on a warm serving plate. Stir cream into sauce; bring almost to a boil. Pour a little sauce over fish. Garnish with parsley. Serve remaining sauce separately.
6. Serve with a dry white wine. Makes 2 servings.

Stuffed Sardines

Sarde Ripiene

---

3 (4-oz.) sardines or smelt, cleaned, page 39
Salt
Freshly ground pepper

Stuffing:
1/4 cup chopped fresh parsley
1 cup fresh bread crumbs
1 tablespoon lemon juice
1 tablespoon grated Parmesan cheese
2 tablespoons butter or margarine, melted
Salt
Freshly ground pepper

To garnish:
Cilantro
Lemon wedges

---

1. Preheat broiler. Wipe fish with paper towels. Sprinkle with salt and pepper.
2. To make stuffing, in a medium bowl, combine parsley, bread crumbs, lemon juice, cheese, butter or margarine, salt and pepper.
3. Fill cavity of each fish with a little stuffing. Place stuffed fish on a broiler-pan rack.
4. Cook stuffed fish 4 to 6 inches from preheated broiler 6 to 8 minutes or until fish turns from translucent to opaque and just begins to flake when pierced with a fork at thickest part, turning once. Serve with Radicchio Salad, page 65, and French-fried potatoes.
5. Serve with a light dry white wine or light red wine. Makes 2 servings.

Venetian-Style Sole

Sogliole alla Veneziana

---

1 (1-1/2-lb.) Dover sole, cleaned, page 39

Savory Butter:
1/4 cup butter or margarine, room temperature
2 teaspoons chopped fresh mint
2 teaspoons chopped fresh parsley
1 garlic clove, crushed
Salt
Freshly ground pepper

Sauce:
2 tablespoons butter or margarine
1 shallot, finely chopped
1/2 cup white wine
Salt
Freshly ground pepper
1/4 cup whipping cream

To garnish:
Parsley sprig

Veal with Tuna Mayonnaise

Vitello Tonnato

---

1 (1-lb.) boneless veal sirloin roast
1 medium onion, quartered
2 whole cloves
1 bay leaf
1 celery stalk, chopped
1 small carrot, chopped
4 peppercorns

Tuna Mayonnaise:
1 egg yolk
2 anchovy fillets, finely chopped
1 tablespoon lemon juice
1 tablespoon capers
1/3 cup olive oil
1 (3-1/2-oz.) can water-pack tuna, drained
Salt
Freshly ground pepper

To serve:
4 anchovy fillets, cut in half lengthwise
About 15 capers
3 lemon slices
1 cilantro sprig

---

1. Place veal in a large saucepan. Add onion, cloves, bay leaf, celery, carrot, peppercorns and enough water to cover.
2. Bring to a boil; skim off any foam. Reduce heat. Cover; simmer 1 hour or until veal is tender. Let veal and liquid cool slightly. Refrigerate veal in liquid until chilled.
3. To make mayonnaise, in a blender, process egg yolk, anchovies, lemon juice and capers until blended.
4. While machine is running, slowly pour in olive oil in a steady stream. Process until all oil is added and mayonnaise is thick and creamy.
5. Add tuna; process until smooth. Season with salt and pepper. If mayonnaise is too thick, blend in a spoonful of cooking liquid from veal.
6. Remove cold veal from cooking liquid, reserving liquid for another use. Cut veal into thin slices. Arrange veal slices on a serving dish. Spread mayonnaise over top of veal, covering completely.
7. Cover dish with foil or plastic wrap; refrigerator at least 8 hours or overnight.
8. To serve, arrange a lattice of anchovies over sauce. Place capers between anchovies; see photo. Garnish with lemon slices and cilantro.
9. Serve with a light dry white wine. Makes 2 servings.

Stuffed Partridges

Pernici Ripiene

---

2 partridges, with livers
Salt
Freshly ground pepper
3/4 cup finely chopped mushrooms (about 2 oz.)
6 bacon slices
3 juniper berries, crushed
2 bread slices, crusts trimmed

To garnish:
Watercress

---

1. Preheat oven to 400F (205C). Rinse partridges; pat dry with paper towels. Sprinkle with salt and pepper.
2. Chop livers finely. In a small bowl, combine chopped livers and mushrooms. Reserve 4 bacon slices; chop remaining 2 bacon slices. Stir chopped bacon, juniper berries, salt and pepper into mushroom mixture.
3. Stuff partridges with mushroom mixture. Wrap 2 bacon slices around each partridge. Place partridges, breast-side up, in a small roasting pan.
4. Roast in preheated oven 35 to 40 minutes or until partridges are tender and juices run clear when pierced between breast and thigh. Remove from pan; keep warm.
5. Discard all but 2 tablespoons pan drippings. Heat drippings on top of stove. Add bread; cook in drippings until crisp and golden, turning once. Place on a warm serving dish; place a roasted partridge on each browned bread slice. Garnish with watercress. Serve with Beans & Mortadella, page 62, and Potato Gnocchi with Parmesan, page 58, or Polenta with Cheese, page 59.
6. Serve with a robust red wine. Makes 2 servings.

Top to bottom: Stuffed Partridges, Veal with Tuna Mayonnaise

Marsala Steaks with Brandy

Bistecchine Casanova

2 (6- to 8-oz.) beef loin sirloin steaks
Salt
Freshly ground pepper
2 tablespoons butter or margarine
2 teaspoons olive oil
3/4 cup finely chopped mushrooms (about 2 oz.)
1 oz. liver pâté
2 tablespoons Marsala
3 tablespoons brandy

To garnish:
2 thyme sprigs or parsley sprigs

1. Sprinkle steaks with salt and pepper.
2. Heat butter or margarine and olive oil in a large skillet. Add seasoned steaks; sauté 2 to 4 minutes on each side until browned and cooked to desired doneness. Transfer to a warm dish; keep warm.
3. Add mushrooms to skillet; cook on high heat 1 minute, stirring constantly. Add pâté and Marsala; stir until combined and hot, breaking up pâté. Season with salt and pepper. Spread mixture over steaks; return to skillet.
4. In a very small saucepan, heat brandy until hot. At the table, pour hot brandy over steaks. Carefully ignite brandy; serve when flames go out. Garnish with thyme or parsley.
5. Serve with a dry red wine or robust red wine. Makes 2 servings.

Left to right: Marsala Steaks with Brandy, Beef Roll with Mushroom Sauce

Beef Roll with Mushroom Sauce

Polpettone alla Toscana

8 oz. lean ground beef
Salt
Freshly ground pepper
1 small onion, chopped
2 bacon slices, finely chopped, blanched
1 tablespoon grated Parmesan cheese
1 garlic clove, crushed
1 egg, beaten
1 cup fresh bread crumbs
1 tablespoon olive oil

Wine Sauce:
1 tablespoon tomato paste
1/2 cup red wine
1/2 cup water
Salt
Freshly ground pepper
1-1/2 cups sliced mushrooms (4 oz.)

1. Place beef in a medium bowl; season with salt and pepper. Add onion, bacon, Parmesan cheese, garlic, egg and 1/2 of bread crumbs. Mix with a fork or your hands until all ingredients are blended.
2. Shape meat mixture into a short roll about 3 inches in diameter. Coat roll with remaining bread crumbs, pressing on crumbs with your fingers. Refrigerate 30 minutes.
3. Heat olive oil in a large, heavy saucepan. Add meat roll; cook about 5 minutes, turning until evenly browned.
4. To make wine sauce, in a small bowl, combine tomato paste, wine, water, salt and pepper. Pour around meat roll; bring to a boil. Reduce heat. Cover; simmer 30 minutes.
5. Add mushrooms to sauce; cook 10 minutes.
6. Remove roll from pan; cut into slices. Pour some of sauce into a serving dish. Arrange meat slices in a row over sauce. Serve any remaining sauce separately. Serve with Beans with Mortadella, page 62, and Potato Gnocchi with Parmesan, page 58, or Polenta with Cheese, page 59.
7. Serve with a robust red wine. Makes 2 servings.

Beef Rolls

Involtine alla Barese

4 (2- to 3-oz.) beef round top round steaks
2 teaspoons chopped fresh parsley
2 teaspoons chopped fresh basil or 1 teaspoon dried leaf basil
1 tablespoon grated Parmesan cheese
1 garlic clove, crushed
Salt
Freshly ground pepper
4 thin cooked ham slices
2 tablespoons olive oil
1 small onion, sliced
1/4 cup red wine
1/4 cup beef stock or water
2 medium tomatoes, peeled, chopped

To garnish:
Parsley sprigs or basil sprigs

1. Place steak slices between 2 sheets of plastic wrap. Pound steak to 1/8 inch thick.
2. In a small bowl, combine parsley, basil, cheese and garlic; set aside.
3. Season pounded steak with salt and pepper; place a ham slice on each steak piece, trimming to fit if necessary.
4. Put a little reserved herb mixture at 1 end of each slice. Roll up steak and ham slices, enclosing herb mixture; secure with wooden picks or kitchen string.
5. Heat olive oil in a large saucepan. Add onion; sauté 5 minutes or until soft. Add beef rolls; sauté 5 minutes or until evenly browned, turning occasionally.
6. Add wine, stock or water and tomatoes. Bring to a boil. Reduce heat. Cover; simmer 1 hour or until meat is tender.
7. Remove rolls from sauce; remove wooden picks or string. Place on a warm serving platter. Pour sauce over rolls. Garnish with parsley or basil. Serve with Sautéed Sunchokes, page 61.
8. Serve with a dry red wine. Makes 2 servings.

Marinated Lamb Pot Roast

Arrosto di Agnello al Ginepro

---

1 (1-1/2-lb.) roast from leg of lamb or shoulder of lamb
1 celery stalk, chopped
1 small carrot, chopped
1 small onion, chopped
6 juniper berries, crushed
1 cup red wine
3 rosemary sprigs or 1/2 teaspoon dried rosemary
2 garlic cloves
1 tablespoon olive oil
Salt
Freshly ground pepper
1 tablespoon red-currant jelly

---

1. Place lamb in a large bowl with celery, carrot, onion, juniper berries, wine, rosemary and garlic. Cover and refrigerate up to 24 hours, turning occasionally.
2. Remove lamb, reserving marinade; pat marinated lamb dry with paper towels.
3. Heat olive oil in a flameproof casserole. Add marinated lamb; cook until browned, turning occasionally. Add reserved marinade.
4. Cover; simmer 1-1/2 hours or until lamb is tender. Remove lamb; place in a warm serving dish. Keep warm.
5. Strain liquid through a sieve; with a wooden spoon, press as much of vegetable mixture through sieve as possible. Return liquid and sieved vegetable mixture to pan; add jelly. Bring to a boil; stir until jelly dissolves.
6. Pour sauce into a serving dish; serve separately.
7. Serve with a fruity medium red or a dry red wine. Makes 2 servings.

Lamb

Lamb shoulder is less expensive than leg of lamb. However, lamb shoulder has more fat marbling. If you want leaner meat, choose a cut from the leg. The leg is also slightly easier to carve than the shoulder.

To carve either roast, you will need a large sharp knife and a carving fork. Lamb is usually carved fairly thickly.

Many people have a preference for rare, medium or well-done meat and would not consider eating meat any other way. The use of a meat thermometer ensures that meat will be cooked perfectly. Beef or lamb can be cooked to rare (140F, 60C), medium (160F, 70C) or well-done (170F, 75C). Both beef and lamb are more juicy and flavorful if not overcooked. Remove roasts from the oven when the internal temperature is 5 to 10 degrees below desired doneness. Roast will continue to cook a few minutes after it is removed from the oven.

Unlike beef or lamb, pork should not be served rare or medium-done. Cook fresh pork to an internal temperature of 170F (75C) for flavor and juciness. Pork should be gray in color with no pink remaining. Although the parasite, trichina, is rarely found in pork today, it is easily destroyed by cooking. Usually trichina is destroyed at 140F (60C).

Left to right: Marinated Lamb Pot Roast, Lamb with Fennel

Pork with Milk & Coriander

Maiale al Latte

2 (1-inch-thick) pork chops
1 teaspoon coriander seeds, crushed
1 teaspoon chopped fresh marjoram or
   1/2 teaspoon dried leaf marjoram
1 garlic clove, finely chopped
2 tablespoons butter or margarine
1 small onion, chopped
1/4 cup finely chopped cooked ham
1 cup milk
Salt
Freshly ground pepper

To garnish:
Cilantro

Cook this recipe over very low heat to keep milk from evaporating. If necessary, add a little more milk and reduce heat.

1. Season chops with coriander, marjoram and garlic.
2. Melt butter or margarine in a saucepan large enough to hold chops in 1 layer. Add chops; cook about 5 minutes or until golden brown, turning once.
3. Remove chops from pan; keep warm. Add onion, ham, milk, salt and pepper to pan; bring to a boil. Reduce heat.
4. Return chops to pan. Adjust heat so mixture barely simmers. Cook about 35 minutes or until chops are tender.
5. Place chops on a warm serving dish; keep warm. Boil sauce 5 minutes or until slightly thickened. Pour a little sauce over chops; serve remaining sauce separately. Garnish with cilantro.
6. Serve with a dry white wine or a light red wine. Makes 2 servings.

Lamb with Fennel

Agnello coi Finocchietti

2 tablespoons olive oil
1 lb. lamb for stew, cut into 1-1/2-inch cubes
1 medium onion, sliced
1 garlic clove, crushed
1 (8-oz.) can tomatoes
1/2 cup beef stock
Salt
Freshly ground black pepper
1 medium fennel bulb with leaves
1 small red or yellow bell pepper, quartered

1. Heat olive oil in a medium saucepan. Add lamb; sauté 5 minutes or until evenly browned, stirring frequently. Add onion and garlic; sauté 5 minutes.
2. Add tomatoes with their liquid, stock, salt and black pepper; bring to a boil. Reduce heat. Cover; simmer 10 minutes.
3. Coarsely chop fennel leaves; reserve for garnish. Cut fennel bulb into thick slices. Add bell pepper and sliced fennel to pan. Cook 30 to 35 minutes or until lamb is tender.
4. Spoon into a serving dish. Garnish with chopped fennel leaves.
5. Serve with a light red wine. Makes 2 servings.

Veal with Vermouth

Scaloppine al Vermouth

1/4 cup all-purpose flour
Salt
Freshly ground pepper
1 lb. veal for stew, cut into 1-inch cubes
2 tablespoons olive oil
1 small onion, chopped
1 tablespoon chopped fresh sage or
   1 teaspoon rubbed sage
2 cups dry vermouth
1 cup chicken stock
1 tablespoon lemon juice
4 oz. whole fresh mushrooms
1 egg yolk
3 tablespoons half and half

To garnish:
Chopped parsley
Sage leaves, if desired

---

1. In a plastic bag, combine flour, salt and pepper. Add veal; toss to coat with seasoned flour. Heat olive oil in a medium saucepan. Add floured veal; sauté about 3 minutes or until evenly browned, stirring frequently. Add onion; sauté 2 minutes.
2. Stir in sage, vermouth and stock; bring to a boil. Add lemon juice, salt and pepper. Reduce heat. Cover; simmer 40 minutes or until veal is tender.
3. Add mushrooms; cook 5 minutes.
4. In a small bowl, stir egg yolk and half and half until smooth. Remove veal from heat; stir egg mixture into sauce. Transfer to a warm serving dish. Garnish with parsley and sage. Serve with rice or pasta and Braised Fennel, page 62.
5. Serve with a fruity dry white wine. Makes 2 servings.

Variation
Substitute pork cubes for veal.

Veal Kabobs

Vitello agli Stecchi

---

8 oz. veal for stew, cut into 1-inch cubes
Salt
Freshly ground pepper
2 tablespoons lemon juice
1 small onion, quartered
4 oz. cooked thin ham slices
Sage leaves
2 tablespoons olive oil

---

1. Preheat oven to 375F (190C). Place veal in a medium bowl. Stir in salt, pepper and lemon juice.
2. Separate onion into layers. Cut ham into 1-inch-wide strips. Wrap a strip of ham around each veal cube. Thread equally onto 2 skewers, alternating with sage leaves and onion pieces. Place skewers in a baking dish; sprinkle with olive oil. Cover with foil.
3. Bake in a preheated oven 25 minutes or until veal is tender. If desired, remove foil for last 5 minutes of cooking; place under broiler for browning. Serve with Rice Pilaf with Mushrooms, page 26, and a tossed salad.
4. Serve with a fruity medium-dry white wine. Makes 2 servings.

Veal

Uncooked veal should be pale in color with no dark or discolored areas. Look for meat which is lean and moist. Cook veal carefully as it toughens quickly when overcooked.

Use turkey as an alternative to veal. Turkey breast is more economical and makes an excellent substitute in most veal dishes. Buy boneless turkey breasts; slice or cube them according to recipe directions. In some markets, turkey-breast cutlets are also available.

Veal Cutlets
with Ham & Cheese

Scaloppine di Vitello alla Vandestana

---

2 tablespoons all-purpose flour
Salt
Freshly ground pepper
2 (4- to 6-oz.) veal cutlets
1 tablespoon olive oil
1 tablespoon butter or margarine
2 oz. prosciutto, chopped
1 teaspoon chopped fresh marjoram or 1/2 teaspoon
dried leaf marjoram
1 tablespoon grated Parmesan cheese
2 tablespoons Marsala

To garnish:
Fresh marjoram

---

1. In a shallow bowl, combine flour, salt and pepper. Dip veal cutlets into seasoned flour until lightly coated.
2. Heat olive oil and butter or margarine in a large skillet. Add floured veal; sauté until golden brown, turning once.
3. Divide prosciutto between browned cutlets; sprinkle with marjoram and cheese. Reduce heat.
4. Pour Marsala around veal; spoon over veal.
5. Cover; simmer 3 to 4 minutes or until cheese melts. Garnish with marjoram.
6. Serve with a light dry white wine. Makes 2 servings.

Top to bottom: Veal with Vermouth, Veal Cutlets with Ham & Cheese

Left to right: Deep-Fried Veal & Vegetables, Veal in Lemon Sauce

Deep-Fried Veal & Vegetables

Fritto Misto

1 (6-oz.) veal cutlet
1 small eggplant
1 small zucchini
4 oz. whole fresh mushrooms
4 thawed frozen or canned artichoke hearts
1/4 cup all-purpose flour
Salt
Freshly ground pepper
2 eggs, beaten
1-1/4 cups dry bread crumbs
Vegetable oil

To garnish:
Lemon wedges

To make dry bread crumbs, spread fresh bread crumbs on a baking sheet; bake in a preheated 250F (120C) oven 30 minutes.

1. Cut veal into 1-inch-wide strips. Slice eggplant thinly. Cut zucchini in half crosswise. Cut halves lengthwise into strips. Wipe mushrooms with a damp paper towel. Drain artichoke hearts on paper towels.
2. In a plastic bag, combine flour, salt and pepper. Add veal strips, eggplant slices, zucchini strips, mushrooms and artichoke hearts; toss to coat in seasoned flour. Dip floured veal and vegetables in eggs; coat with bread crumbs, pressing crumbs on with your fingers. Refrigerate 30 minutes to set coating.
3. Heat oil in a large saucepan to 350F (175C) or until a 1-inch bread cube turns golden brown in 65 seconds.
4. Deep-fry veal and vegetables, a few at a time, 3 minutes or until crisp and golden brown. Drain on paper towels; keep warm. Garnish with lemon wedges. Serve with a tossed salad.
5. Serve with a dry white or light red wine. Makes 2 servings.

1. Season chops with salt and pepper. Dip in egg; coat with bread crumbs, pressing crumbs on with your fingers. Refrigerate 15 minutes to set crumbs.
2. Heat 2 teaspoons olive oil in a small saucepan. Add garlic; sauté 2 minutes. Add tomatoes, marjoram, salt and pepper. Reduce heat. Simmer 12 to 15 minutes or until tomatoes are soft, stirring occasionally.
3. Meanwhile, cook chops. Heat 1 tablespoon olive oil and butter or margarine in a large skillet. Add coated chops; sauté 12 to 15 minutes or until golden brown, turning once.
4. Place chops on a warm serving dish; pour sauce over chops or serve separately.
5. Serve with a dry white wine or a light red wine. Makes 2 servings.

Veal in Lemon Sauce

Scaloppine di Vitello al Limone

---

2 tablespoons all-purpose flour
Salt
Freshly ground pepper
1 (12-oz.) veal fillet, thinly sliced
1 tablespoon olive oil
2 tablespoons butter or margarine
2 tablespoons lemon juice
2 tablespoons chicken stock or water

To garnish:
2 tablespoons chopped fresh parsley
Lemon wedges

---

1. In a shallow bowl, combine flour, salt and pepper. Add veal; coat with seasoned flour. Heat olive oil and 1 tablespoon butter or margarine in a medium skillet. Add floured veal; sauté about 2 minutes or until lightly browned, turning once. Remove veal from skillet; keep warm.
2. Reduce heat; stir lemon juice and stock or water into skillet, scraping up any browned bits. Season with salt and pepper. Add remaining 1 tablespoon butter or margarine to skillet; stir until melted.
3. Return veal to skillet; heat in sauce. Place veal on a warm serving dish; spoon any remaining sauce over veal. Sprinkle with chopped parsley. Garnish with lemon slices.
4. Serve with a dry white wine. Makes 2 servings.

Variation
Substitute pork loin tenderloin for veal. Prepare as above.

Veal Chops with Tomatoes & Marjoram

Cotolette alla Milaniese

---

2 (1/2-inch-thick) veal loin top loin chops
Salt
Freshly ground pepper
1 egg, beaten
1 cup fresh bread crumbs
2 teaspoons olive oil
1 garlic clove, crushed
2 medium tomatoes, peeled, chopped
2 teaspoons chopped fresh marjoram or 1 teaspoon
   dried leaf marjoram
1 tablespoon olive oil
2 tablespoons butter or margarine

Chicken Baked with Peppers

Pollo Arrosto con Peperoni

---

2 chicken pieces
2 garlic cloves, crushed
2 rosemary sprigs or 1/2 teaspoon dried rosemary
1 small red bell pepper, cut into 8 strips
1 small green bell pepper, cut into 8 strips
1 tablespoon olive oil
Salt
Freshly ground black pepper
3 tablespoons white wine

To garnish:
Cilantro

---

1. Preheat oven to 375F (190C). Place chicken in a small baking dish. Add garlic and rosemary.
2. Place bell peppers around chicken; drizzle with olive oil. Season with salt and black pepper. Pour wine into dish. Cover with a lid or foil.
3. Bake in preheated oven 35 to 40 minutes or until juices run clear when pierced with a fork. After 25 minutes, remove cover to brown chicken.
4. Place chicken on a warm serving dish; surround with bell peppers. Garnish with cilantro.
5. Serve with a dry white wine. Makes 2 servings.

Stuffed Chicken Breasts

Petti di Pollo Ripieni

---

2 chicken-breast halves
3 tablespoons butter or margarine, room temperature
1/4 cup finely chopped cooked ham
1 garlic clove, crushed
1 tablespoon grated Parmesan cheese
1/2 teaspoon dried rosemary
Salt
Freshly ground pepper
3 tablespoons white wine

To garnish:
Rosemary sprigs, if desired

---

1. Preheat oven to 400F (205C). With your fingers, gently loosen skin from cut sides of chicken; leave attached on uncut sides. Set aside.
2. In a small bowl, combine 2 tablespoons butter or margarine, ham, garlic, Parmesan cheese, rosemary, salt and pepper to make a stuffing.
3. Spread 1/2 of stuffing under skin of 1 chicken breast; secure skin with wooden picks. Repeat with remaining stuffing and chicken.
4. Place stuffed chicken in a small baking dish. Dot with remaining 1 tablespoon butter or margarine. Season with salt and pepper.

5. Bake in preheated oven 30 to 35 minutes or until golden brown and juices run clear when pierced with a fork. Place chicken in a warm serving dish. Pour pan juices into a small saucepan. Add wine; bring to a boil. Simmer 2 minutes.
6. Pour sauce over chicken. Garnish with rosemary, if desired.
7. Serve with a dry white wine. Makes 2 servings.

 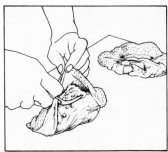

1/With your fingers, gently loosen skin from cut sides of chicken. Leave skin attached on uncut side.

2/Spread 1/2 of stuffing under skin of each chicken breast; secure skin with wooden picks.

Left to right: Chicken Baked with Peppers, Stuffed Chicken Breasts, Chicken with Piquant Green Sauce

Chicken with Piquant Green Sauce

Pollo con Salse Verde

2 chicken-breast halves
1 celery stalk, chopped
1 small carrot, chopped
1 small onion, quartered
6 peppercorns
2 whole cloves

Piquant Green Sauce:
1 garlic clove, crushed
1 tablespoon capers, finely chopped
1/2 cup finely chopped fresh parsley
1 tablespoon wine vinegar
1/2 teaspoon Dijon-style mustard
6 tablespoons olive oil
Salt
Freshly ground pepper

To garnish:
Lemon wedges

Use stock from cooking chicken for soups or sauces.

1. Place chicken in a medium saucepan. Add celery, carrot, onion, peppercorns, cloves and enough water to cover.
2. Bring to a boil. Reduce heat. Cover; simmer 25 to 30 minutes or until chicken is tender. Remove chicken from stock; reserve stock for another use, if desired. Cover and refrigerate chicken until chilled or up to 8 hours.
3. To make sauce, in a small bowl, combine garlic, capers, parsley, vinegar and mustard. Gradually stir in olive oil; season with salt and pepper.
4. Thinly slice chilled chicken breasts; arrange on a serving dish. Pour a little green sauce over each slice; serve any remaining sauce separately. Garnish with lemon wedges. Serve with Bean Salad with Chive Dressing, page 67, and hard rolls.
5. Serve with a dry white wine or light red wine. Makes 2 servings.

Chicken Livers with Sage & Wine

Salsa di Fegatini

12 oz. chicken livers
2 tablespoons butter or margarine
1 small onion, finely chopped
6 whole sage leaves or 1 teaspoon rubbed sage
Salt
Freshly ground pepper
1/2 cup white wine

To garnish:
Sage leaves
10 orange slices, halved

1. Rinse chicken livers; pat dry with paper towels.
2. Melt butter or margarine in a small skillet. Add onion; sauté 5 minutes or until soft, stirring occasionally.
3. Add rinsed and dried chicken livers and sage; sauté 3 to 4 minutes or until livers are lightly browned on all sides, stirring.
4. Season with salt and pepper; pour in wine. Bring to a boil. Reduce heat. Simmer 6 to 8 minutes or until chicken livers are slightly pink in center.
5. Spoon into a warm serving dish. Garnish with sage and orange slices. Serve with Potato Gnocchi with Parmesan, page 58, or Rice Pilaf with Mushrooms, page 26, and a green vegetable.
6. Serve with a robust red wine. Makes 2 servings.

Duck in Sweet & Sour Sauce

Anitra in Agrodolce

2 duck-breast halves, thawed if frozen
2 tablespoons butter or margarine
1 large onion, thinly sliced
1 cup chicken stock
1 tablespoon wine vinegar
1 tablespoon honey
Salt
Freshly ground pepper
2 tablespoons raisins
1 tablespoon chopped fresh mint or
   1 teaspoon dried leaf mint
1/4 cup pine nuts

To garnish:
Mint leaves

1. Trim and discard excess fat from duck. Melt butter or margarine in a medium saucepan. Add duck; sauté about 10 minutes, turning until evenly browned.
2. Remove duck from pan; add onion. Sauté 5 minutes or until soft.
3. Add stock, vinegar, honey, salt and pepper. Bring to a boil; return duck to pan. Reduce heat.
4. Cover; simmer 45 minutes or until duck is tender. Ten minutes before end of cooking time, add raisins, mint and pine nuts.
5. Remove duck from sauce; place in a warm serving dish. Skim fat from top of sauce with a spoon; pour sauce over duck.
6. Garnish with mint leaves. Serve with Potato Gnocchi with Parmesan, page 58, and a tossed salad.
7. Serve with a light dry while or light red wine. Makes 2 servings.

Calves' Liver with Onions

Fegato alla Veneziana

8 oz. calves' liver, thinly sliced
Salt
Freshly ground pepper
1 tablespoon lemon juice
3 tablespoons olive oil
1 large onion, sliced
2 teaspoons all-purpose flour
1/4 cup red wine
1 tablespoon chopped fresh parsley

1. Rinse liver; pat dry with paper towels. In a medium bowl, season liver with salt, pepper and lemon juice; set aside.
2. Heat olive oil in a large skillet. Add onion; sauté 10 minutes or until lightly browned.
3. Dust seasoned liver lightly with flour; add floured liver to skillet. Sauté about 5 minutes or until lightly browned, turning once.
4. Add wine, parsley, salt and pepper. Reduce heat. Simmer 5 minutes, stirring onions and turning liver. Do not overcook; liver should still be slightly pink in center. Serve hot.
5. Serve with Scalloped Potatoes, page 63, and a green vegetable.
6. Serve with a light red wine. Makes 2 servings.

Clockwise from left: Chicken Livers with Sage & Wine, Green salad, Duck in Sweet & Sour Sauce

Vegetables & Salads

Mushrooms with Mint

Funghi Porcini al Tegame

1/4 cup butter or margarine
12 oz. small whole mushrooms (about 3 cups)
1 tablespoon chopped fresh mint
1 tablespoon lemon juice
2 tablespoons red wine or beef stock
Salt
Freshly ground pepper

1. Melt butter or margarine in a medium saucepan. Add mushrooms; sauté about 5 minutes or until softened.
2. Stir in mint, lemon juice, wine or stock, salt and pepper. Cover; simmer 10 minutes or until mushrooms are tender and pan juices evaporate. Spoon into a warm serving dish. Serve hot. Makes 2 servings.

Asparagus with Egg

Asparagi all'Italiana

8 oz. asparagus spears
2 tablespoons half and half
2 teaspoons lemon juice
Salt
Freshly ground pepper
1 egg
1 teaspoon grated Parmesan cheese

1. Break off tough ends of asparagus spears. Pour 2 to 3 inches of water into a wide shallow saucepan. Bring to a boil. Add asparagus; return to a boil. Reduce heat. Cover; simmer asparagus 10 minutes or until tender. Drain; place on a warm serving dish. Keep warm.
2. In a small bowl, combine half and half, lemon juice, salt and pepper. Set aside.
3. Pour 1 inch of water into a small shallow saucepan; add salt. Bring to a simmer. Break egg into a cup; slide egg from cup into simmering water. Poach egg about 3 minutes or until white is just set.
4. Remove egg with a slotted spoon; place on asparagus. Spoon half-and-half mixture over egg; sprinkle with Parmesan cheese. Serve hot. To serve, divide egg and asparagus into 2 servings. Makes 2 servings.

Variation
For a heartier dish, poach 2 eggs.

Green-Pea Soufflés

Sformato di Piselli

1-1/2 cups fresh or thawed frozen green peas
2 tablespoons butter or margarine
1 small onion, finely chopped
1/4 cup finely chopped cooked ham
2 tablespoons all-purpose flour
1/2 cup milk
Salt
Freshly ground pepper
2 eggs, separated

1. Preheat oven to 400F (205C). Butter 2 (1-1/2- to 2-cup) ovenproof dishes. Cook peas in boiling salted water until tender; drain. Set aside.
2. Melt butter or margarine in a small saucepan. Add onion; sauté 5 minutes or until soft. Stir in ham and flour; cook 1 minute, stirring constantly.
3. Gradually stir in milk; stir until sauce is thickened. Season with salt and pepper.
4. Cool slightly; beat in egg yolks. Stir in cooked peas.
5. In a small bowl, beat egg whites until stiff but not dry. Stir 1 tablespoon beaten egg white into sauce; fold in remaining beaten egg whites. Divide mixture between buttered dishes.
6. Bake in preheated oven about 25 minutes or until soufflés are puffed and golden brown. Serve immediately. Makes 2 servings.

Top to bottom: Green-Pea Soufflés, Asparagus with Egg

Potato Gnocchi with Parmesan

Gnocchi di Patate

1 lb. baking potatoes, peeled (2 to 3 medium potatoes)
3/4 cup plus 2 tablespoons all-purpose flour
1 egg, beaten
2 tablespoons butter or margarine
Salt
Freshly ground pepper
1 tablespoon grated Parmesan cheese

Gnocchi can be served as a simple first course or as a side dish as an alternative to rice or pasta. It is particularly good with game and rich meat dishes, such as Duck in Sweet & Sour Sauce, page 55.

1. Cut each potato in 2 or 3 pieces. Cook potatoes in boiling salted water 15 to 20 minutes or until tender. Drain well. Place drained potatoes in a medium bowl; mash until smooth.
2. Stir flour, egg, 1 tablespoon butter or margarine, salt and pepper into potatoes until combined. On a lightly floured surface; knead potato mixture lightly.
3. Divide dough into 2 equal pieces. Roll each piece into a roll about 3/4 inch in diameter. Cut into 1-inch pieces.
4. Meanwhile, bring a large saucepan of salted water to a boil. Add 1/2 of gnocchi; boil at least 3 minutes or until gnocchi rise to top. Remove with a slotted spoon; place in a warm serving dish. Keep warm. Repeat with remaining gnocchi.
5. Dot gnocchi with remaining 1 tablespoon butter or margarine; sprinkle with Parmesan cheese. Serve immediately. Makes 2 servings.

Spinach with Egg

Crocchette di Spinaci

1 hard-cooked egg
1 lb. fresh spinach or 1 (10-oz) pkg. frozen leaf
  spinach
2 tablespoons butter or margarine
Ground nutmeg
Salt
Freshly ground pepper
1 tablespoon lemon juice

1. Cut egg in half; remove and reserve yolk. Chop white; set aside.
2. Wash fresh spinach; remove large stems. Place washed spinach in a large saucepan with only water that clings to leaves. Cover; cook 7 to 10 minutes, shaking pan occasionally, or until spinach is tender. Cook frozen spinach according to package directions.

Left to right: Spinach with Egg, Potato Gnocchi with Parmesan, Polenta with Cheese

3. Drain cooked spinach; return to saucepan. Add butter or margarine; season with nutmeg, salt and pepper. Heat through; remove from heat. Stir in chopped egg white and lemon juice.
4. Place spinach mixture in a warm serving dish; sieve reserved egg yolk over top. Serve hot. Makes 2 servings.

Polenta with Cheese

Polenta con Formaggio

1 cup water
Pinch of salt
1/3 cup cornmeal
2 tablespoons butter or margarine
2 tablespoons grated Parmesan cheese

Polenta is a popular alternative to rice or pasta in Northern Italy. It goes well with rich, well-flavored dishes.

1. Bring water to boil in a medium saucepan. Add salt; stir in cornmeal with a large wooden spoon. Cook, stirring, about 25 minutes or until thickened and smooth.
2. Dampen a flat plate or tray. Pour polenta onto damp plate or tray; spread to 1/2 inch thick. Let cool to room temperature.
3. Cut polenta into 1/2-inch cubes. Heat butter or margarine in a medium skillet until foaming. Add polenta; sauté about 5 minutes or until browned, stirring carefully.
4. Stir in Parmesan cheese; heat until cheese just melts. Spoon into a warm serving dish; serve immediately. Makes 2 servings.

Deep-Fried Artichoke Hearts

Carciofi Fritti

5 or 6 canned artichoke hearts
5 tablespoons all-purpose flour
Salt
Freshly ground pepper
1 egg, separated
1 tablespoon olive oil
1/2 cup water
Vegetable oil

1. Drain artichoke hearts; cut into quarters. Set aside. In a medium bowl, combine flour, salt and pepper. Stir in egg yolk, olive oil and water to form a stiff batter.
2. In a small bowl, beat egg white until soft peaks form. Fold beaten egg white into batter.
3. In a large deep saucepan, heat 4 inches of vegetable oil to 350F (175C) or until a 1-inch bread cube turns golden brown in 65 seconds. Dip quartered artichoke hearts in batter; deep-fry in hot oil, a few at a time, 2 to 3 minutes or until golden brown.
4. Drain on paper towels; serve hot. Makes 2 servings.

Sautéed Sunchokes

Frittura di Carciofi di Giudea

1 lb. sunchokes (Jerusalem artichokes), peeled
2 tablespoons lemon juice
2 tablespoons olive oil
1 garlic clove, crushed

To garnish:
Chopped fresh parsley

1. Place sunchokes in a medium saucepan. Add lemon juice and enough water to cover. Bring to a boil. Reduce heat. Simmer 10 minutes or until crisp-tender. Drain; cool slightly. Cut sunchokes into thin slices. Pat slices dry with paper towels.
2. Heat olive oil in a medium skillet. Add garlic; sauté 2 minutes. Add sunchoke slices; sauté until golden brown and tender.
3. Spoon into a warm serving dish. Sprinkle parsley over top; stir carefully to avoid breaking sunchoke slices. Serve hot. Makes 2 servings.

Tomato & Mozzarella Salad

Insalata di Mozzarella e Pomodoro

1 large or 2 small tomatoes, thinly sliced
3 oz. mozzarella cheese, thinly sliced
4 or 5 basil leaves, chopped
Dressing:
1 tablespoon tarragon vinegar
2 tablespoons olive oil
Salt
Freshly ground pepper
1 garlic clove, crushed

1. Arrange tomatoes and cheese alternately on a serving plate. Sprinkle with basil.
2. To make dressing, place all ingredients in a small container with a tight-fitting lid. Cover tightly. Shake to combine; pour over salad. Salad can be covered and refrigerated up to 4 hours before serving. Makes 2 servings.

Carrots in Marsala

Carote al Marsala

2 large carrots
1 tablespoon olive oil
Salt
Freshly ground pepper
1/4 cup Marsala

To garnish:
Chopped fresh parsley

1. Cut carrots in half crosswise. Cut carrot halves into 1/4-inch wide sticks. Heat olive oil in a medium saucepan. Add carrot sticks; stir to coat with oil.
2. Add salt, pepper and Marsala; bring to a boil. Reduce heat. Cover; simmer about 10 minutes or until carrots are crisp-tender. Arrange in a warm serving dish. Sprinkle with parsley; serve hot or at room temperature. Makes 2 servings.

Clockwise from top left: Deep-Fried Artichoke Hearts, Sautéed Sunchokes, Tomato & Mozzarella Salad

Left to right: Braised Fennel, Celery with Ham

Braised Fennel

Finocchi Stufati

2 small or 1 large fennel bulb, quartered
1 tablespoon lemon juice
1/2 cup hot chicken stock
1/2 cup fresh bread crumbs
1 tablespoon grated Parmesan cheese
1 teaspoon finely grated lemon peel
Salt
Freshly ground pepper
2 tablespoons butter or margarine

1. Preheat oven to 375F (190C). Butter a small baking dish.
2. Trim off any tough stalks and bottom from fennel. Add trimmed fennel and lemon juice to boiling salted water. Cook 10 minutes; drain.
3. Place boiled fennel in buttered dish; add hot stock. In a small bowl, combine bread crumbs, cheese, lemon peel, salt and pepper. Sprinkle over boiled fennel.
4. Bake in preheated oven 30 to 35 minutes or until fennel is tender and topping is golden brown. Makes 2 servings.

Beans with Mortadella

Fave alla Mortadella

1-1/2 lb. broad beans in pods, shelled
1 celery stalk, chopped
2 thick Mortadella slices
2 tablespoons butter or margarine
Salt
Freshly ground pepper

1. Place a steamer rack in a medium saucepan. Add enough water to almost touch bottom of steamer. Bring to a boil; add beans and celery to rack. Steam 15 minutes or until tender. Remove from heat; keep warm.
2. Cut Mortadella into thin strips. Melt butter or margarine in a medium skillet. Add Mortadella strips; sauté 3 minutes or until hot.
3. Stir in steamed vegetables. Season with salt and pepper. Cook 3 minutes to blend flavors. Serve hot. Makes 2 servings.

Variation
Substitute lima beans for broad beans.

Celery with Ham

Sedano al Forno

---

4 celery stalks
Salt
2 tablespoons butter or margarine
1 small onion, sliced
1/4 cup diced cooked ham
3 bay leaves
Freshly ground pepper
1/2 cup chicken stock

---

1. Cut each celery stalk into 3 pieces. Cook in boiling salted water 10 minutes; drain. Set aside.
2. Melt butter or margarine in a medium saucepan. Add onion; sauté 5 minutes or until soft. Add ham; cook 1 minute.
3. Add boiled celery, bay leaves, pepper and stock. Bring to a boil. Reduce heat. Cover; simmer 12 to 15 minutes or until celery is tender. Spoon into a warm serving dish. Discard bay leaves. Serve hot. Makes 2 servings.

Scalloped Potatoes

Patate al Forno

2-1/4 cups thinly sliced potatoes (about 2 medium)
1 small onion, thinly sliced
Salt
Freshly ground pepper
Ground nutmeg
2 tablespoons butter or margarine
1/2 cup half and half
1 tablespoon grated Parmesan cheese

---

1. Preheat oven to 400F (205C). Butter a 1-quart baking dish. Layer potatoes and onion in buttered dish. Season each layer with salt, pepper and nutmeg; dot top with butter or margarine.
2. Pour half and half over potatoes and onions. Sprinkle with cheese.
3. Bake uncovered in preheated oven 40 to 45 minutes or until potatoes are tender and top is golden brown. Serve hot. Makes 2 servings.

Left to right: Belgian Endive with Hazelnut Dressing, Radicchio
Salad

Belgian Endive
with Hazelnut Dressing

Insalata di Cicoria

---

2 Belgian-endive heads

Hazelnut Dressing:
2 tablespoons coarsely chopped hazelnuts
Salt
Freshly ground pepper
1 tablespoon lemon juice
3 tablespoons half and half
1 garlic clove, crushed

To garnish:
2 teaspoons chopped fresh parsley

---

1. Separate endive leaves; arrange around edge of a shallow dish. Set aside.
2. To make dressing, in a small bowl, beat dressing ingredients lightly with a fork to combine; pour dressing over endive tips in center of dish.
3. Sprinkle parsley over dressing. Makes 2 servings.

1. Cut bread into 1/2-inch cubes. Heat 3 tablespoons olive oil in a medium skillet. Add garlic; sauté 1 minute. Add bread cubes; sauté about 5 minutes or until golden brown. Drain on paper towels; let cool to room temperature. Garlic croutons can be made several days ahead; store in a tightly covered container.

2. Place remaining 2 tablespoons olive oil, salt, pepper and vinegar in a container with a tight-fitting lid. Cover tightly. Shake to combine.

3. Finely shred radicchio; place in a serving dish. Sprinkle with mushrooms and croutons. Pour dressing over salad just before serving, shaking to recombine. Garnish with parsley. Makes 2 servings.

Tomato-Stuffed Eggplant

Melanzane Ripiene

---

1 small eggplant
2 tablespoons olive oil
1 garlic clove, crushed
1 small onion, chopped
2 medium tomatoes, peeled, chopped
1/2 to 1 teaspoon dried leaf oregano
Salt
Freshly ground pepper
2 teaspoons grated Parmesan cheese
1 tablespoon chopped fresh parsley

Served hot or cold, this dish also makes an excellent starter. It can be kept warm in the oven up to 30 minutes, if necessary.

1. Preheat oven to 350F (175C). Grease a baking pan. Cut eggplant in half lengthwise. Scoop out inside, leaving 1/2 inch in shell. Reserve scooped-out flesh. Place eggplant shells in greased baking pan; brush insides with a little oil.

2. Bake in preheated oven 15 minutes or until soft.

3. Meanwhile, finely chop reserved eggplant flesh. Heat oil in a medium saucepan over medium-high heat. Add garlic and onion; sauté 5 minutes or until soft.

4. Add chopped eggplant and tomatoes. Season with oregano, salt and pepper. Stir well. Reduce heat. Simmer 10 minutes.

5. Divide tomato mixture between baked eggplant shells. Sprinkle with Parmesan cheese and parsley.

6. Bake filled shells 15 to 20 minutes or until filling bubbles. Serve hot or cold. To serve cold, cool slightly; cover and refrigerate until chilled or up to 2 days. Makes 2 servings.

Radicchio Salad

Insalata di Radicchio

---

2 bread slices
5 tablespoons olive oil
1 garlic clove, crushed
Salt
Freshly ground pepper
2 teaspoons wine vinegar
1 small head radicchio
3/4 cup sliced mushrooms (about 2 oz.)

To garnish:
Parsley sprigs

Beet & Radish Salad

Insalata di Bietola e Ravanelli

---

2 medium raw beets, peeled, finely grated (about 2-1/2
  cups)
4 or 5 red-onion slices, separated into rings
5 or 6 radishes, thinly sliced

Dressing:
2 tablespoons olive oil
1 tablespoon red-wine vinegar
1/2 teaspoon dry mustard
Pinch of sugar
Salt
Freshly ground pepper
1 teaspoon chopped fresh mint, if desired

To garnish:
Fresh mint, if desired

---

1. Place beets in a serving bowl; top with onion. Arrange radishes over top of salad
2. To make dressing, place all ingredients in a small container with a tight-fitting lid. Cover tightly. Shake to combine.
3. Pour dressing over salad just before serving. Garnish with mint, if desired. Makes 2 servings.

Cucumber Salad with Honey

Cetriolo al Miele

1/2 cucumber, cut into small cubes
Salt
2 green onions, finely chopped

Dressing:
2 teaspoons honey
2 teaspoons lemon juice
2 tablespoons olive oil
1/2 teaspoon chopped fresh marjoram or 1/4 teaspoon
  dried leaf marjoram, if desired
Freshly ground pepper

To garnish:
Green-onion flower, see box at right

---

1. Place cucumber in a colander over a bowl; sprinkle with salt. Let stand 30 minutes to drain off excess liquid. Rinse; pat dry with paper towels.
2. In a salad bowl, combine drained cucumber and onions. To make dressing, in a small bowl, combine all ingredients. Pour over cucumber and onions; toss to coat with dressing.
3. Garnish with green-onion flower. Makes 2 servings.

Bean Salad with Chive Dressing

Insalata di Fagiolini

---

8 oz. fresh green beans

Chive Dressing:
1 tablespoon wine vinegar
2 tablespoons olive oil
1 tablespoon chopped chives
1 garlic clove, crushed
Freshly ground pepper
1/2 teaspoon dry mustard
Pinch of sugar
Salt

---

1. Place a steamer rack in a medium saucepan. Add enough water to almost touch bottom of steamer. Bring to a boil; add beans. Steam 7 to 10 minutes or until crisp-tender. Rinse beans under cold running water to cool beans and stop cooking. Drain; place in a serving bowl.
2. To make dressing, place all ingredients in a small container with a tight-fitting lid. Cover tightly. Shake to combine.
3. Pour dressing over beans. Serve immediately or cover and refrigerate up to 24 hours. Bring to room temperature before serving. Makes 2 servings.

Green Salads

A green salad can be a simple but delicious addition to a meal. Instead of iceberg lettuce, use leaf lettuce, radicchio, spinach or Chinese cabbage. For added crunch, add slices or small pieces of celery, bell pepper, cabbage, cucumber or lightly cooked green beans.

To garnish a salad attractively, top it with zesty croutons, fresh herbs, grated carrots or a green-onion flower.

To make a green-onion flower, trim top and bottom from a green onion, leaving a 3-inch stalk. With a sharp knife, shred white part to within 1 inch of green top. Place in iced water at least 1 hour or overnight. The shredded part will open into a flower.

Clockwise from left: Beet & Radish Salad with dressing, Cucumber Salad with Honey, Bean Salad with Chive Dressing

Desserts

Pistachio Ice Cream

Gelato al Pistacchio

---

2 egg yolks
1/4 cup sugar
1/2 cup milk
1/3 cup finely chopped pistachios
1/4 cup whipping cream
Green food coloring, if desired

To decorate:
Chopped pistachios

To serve:
Cookies

---

1. In a small bowl, beat egg yolks and sugar until lemon-colored. In a small saucepan, heat milk until small bubbles form around edge of pan. Gradually stir hot milk into egg-yolk mixture.
2. Pour milk mixture into saucepan used to heat milk; add pistachios. Cook over low heat about 10 minutes, stirring, or until slightly thickened.
3. Cool slightly. Cover surface of custard with a sheet of waxed paper; refrigerate until chilled.
4. In a small bowl, whip cream until soft peaks form; fold whipped cream into chilled custard. Add a few drops of green food coloring, if desired.
5. Pour custard into a 9" x 5" loaf pan; freeze about 1-1/2 hours or until almost firm. Place in a large bowl; beat until light and fluffy.
6. Return to loaf pan; freeze 1-1/2 to 2-1/2 hours or until firm.
7. To serve, place ice cream in refrigerator 30 minutes before serving. Spoon into 2 individual dishes. Decorate with pistachios. Serve with cookies. Makes 2 servings.

Almond Cream Cheese with Strawberries

Crema di Mascarpone

---

2 tablespoons sugar
1/2 (8-oz.) pkg. cream cheese, room temperature
1 tablespoon ground almonds
1 tablespoon Cointreau
1-1/2 cups sliced fresh strawberries

---

1. In a small bowl, beat sugar and cream cheese until smooth and creamy.
2. Gradually beat in ground almonds; beat in Cointreau.
3. Spoon mixture into center of 2 individual plates, or press mixture into a small heart-shaped mold. Place a serving plate over mold. Invert mold; remove.
4. Serve immediately, or cover and refrigerate up to 24 hours. Arrange strawberries around cheese. Makes 2 servings.

Chocolate & Pear Trifles

Zuppa Inglese

---

1 (8-oz.) can pears, packed in juice
4 ladyfingers, each broken into 4 pieces
1 oz. semisweet chocolate, chopped
2 tablespoons Marsala
1/2 cup prepared custard or vanilla pudding
1/2 cup whipping cream

To decorate:
Chocolate curls

Use leftover custard for this or make custard from your favorite recipe or mix. If time is short, use one of the canned puddings; thin with a little milk, if necessary.

1. Drain pears, reserving juice. Chop pears; place chopped pears in 2 individual dishes. Divide ladyfingers between dishes. Pour 2 tablespoons pear juice over ladyfingers in each dish.
2. Place chocolate and Marsala in a very small saucepan; stir over low heat until chocolate melts. Cool slightly. Stir in custard. Spoon into dishes. Cover and refrigerate until chilled or up to 24 hours.
3. To serve, in a small bowl, whip cream until soft peaks form. Spoon over chocolate custard.
4. Decorate with chocolate curls. Makes 2 servings.

Top to bottom: Pistachio Ice Cream with cookies, Almond Cream Cheese with Strawberries

Italian Fruit Salad

Italian Fruit Salad

Macedonia di Frutta

2 medium oranges
1/2 medium lemon
1 firm, ripe medium pear or 1 medium apple, peeled
2 firm, ripe large apricots
1 firm, ripe medium peach
1/2 cup seedless grapes
2 tablespoons Maraschino liqueur or kirsch
1 tablespoon sugar

To serve:
Sugar
1 small banana

Choose any fruits that are in season. However, avoid very soft fruits because they tend to become mushy when marinated.

1. Squeeze juice from oranges into a medium bowl. Finely grate lemon peel; squeeze juice into bowl.
2. Quarter and core apple or pear. Cut cored fruit into small cubes. Add to bowl; stir to coat with juice.
3. Pit and peel apricots and peach; cut peeled apricots and peach into cubes. Add apricot and peach cubes and grapes to bowl.
4. Stir in liqueur and sugar. Place a small plate over fruit salad to hold fruit under juice. Marinate in refrigerator 3 hours or overnight.
5. To serve, make a mound of sugar in a small flat dish. Dip rims of 2 large wine glasses in water; dip them quickly in sugar.
6. Slice banana into fruit salad; stir to distribute. Spoon into sugared glasses. Makes 2 servings.

Rum & Chocolate Dessert

Il Diplomatico

1/4 (1-lb.) pound cake
2 tablespoons dark rum
1/2 cup hot double-strength coffee
1 tablespoon sugar
2 oz. semisweet chocolate, chopped
1 egg, separated

To serve:
1/2 pint whipping cream
Crystallized fruit

---

1. Cut cake into thin slices. Lightly butter 2 small bowls or large cups. Line bowls or cups with cake slices, cutting pieces to fit. Reserve enough cake to cover bowls.
2. In a small bowl, combine rum, coffee and sugar. Stir until sugar dissolves. Sprinkle mixture over cake in bowls, reserving a little for top.
3. Melt chocolate in a very small saucepan over very low heat. Cool slightly; stir in egg yolk. In a small bowl, beat egg white until stiff but not dry. Fold beaten egg white into chocolate mixture. Pour into cake-lined bowls or cups.
4. Cover chocolate mixture with remaining cake; sprinkle cake with reserved coffee mixture. Cover and refrigerate overnight.
5. To serve, place a small plate over each dessert; invert. Remove bowls or cups. In a medium bowl, whip cream until stiff peaks form. Spoon into a pastry bag fitted with a rosette tip. Pipe whipped-cream rosettes completely over each dessert. Decorate top with crystallized fruit. Makes 2 servings.

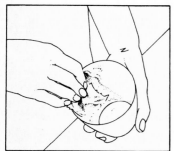

1/Lightly butter 2 small bowls or large cups.

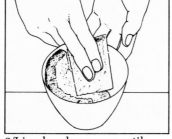

2/Line bowls or cups wtih cake slices, cutting pieces to fit.

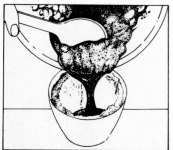

3/Pour chocolate mixture into cake-lined bowls or cups.

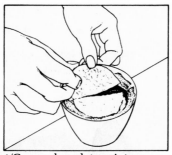

4/Cover chocolate mixture with remaining cake.

Rum & Chocolate Dessert

Marinated Oranges in Curaçao

Arance al Curaçao

---

3 medium oranges
2 tablespoons sugar
1 tablespoon lemon juice
3 tablespoons curaçao or Cointreau

---

1. Cut 1 orange in half. Cut colored peel from 1 orange half; do not include any white pith. Cut peel into thin strips. Place strips in a small saucepan. Cover with water. Simmer 5 minutes; drain. Rinse under cold running water. Pat dry.
2. Using a sharp knife, remove peel and white pith from all oranges, following steps below. Cut peeled oranges into thin slices; place orange slices and blanched peel in a serving dish.
3. Add sugar, lemon juice and liqueur; stir carefully. Cover and refrigerate at least 2 hours or overnight. Spoon into 2 dishes. Makes 2 servings.

Pears Poached in Marsala & Orange

Pere Affogate a Marsala

---

2 or 3 firm, ripe medium pears
1/4 cup Marsala
3/4 cup orange juice
3 tablespoons whipping cream

---

1. Peel pears. Cut in quarters or halves; remove cores.
2. Place pears in a medium saucepan. Add Marsala and orange juice; simmer 10 to 15 minutes or until pears are tender.
3. Remove pan from heat; stir in cream. Arrange cooked pears and cooking liquid in a serving dish. Serve warm. Makes 2 servings.

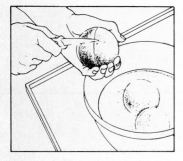

1/To remove orange peel and white pith easily, score the orange into 4 sections. Place scored oranges in boiling water 30 seconds.

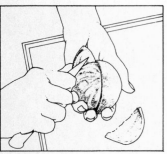

2/Using a knife, pull off peel. Remove as much white pith as possible.

3/Using a sharp knife, cut peeled oranges into thin slices.

Left to right: Pears Poached in Marsala & Orange, Orange Sorbet

Orange Sorbet

Granita di Arancia

2 large oranges
1/4 cup sugar
2 tablespoons water
1 egg white
2 tablespoons sugar

To decorate:
Mint leaves

If there's more sorbet than will fit in the orange shells, cover and freeze for another occasion.

1. Cut off 1-1/2 inches from tops off oranges; using a teaspoon or a grapefruit knife, scoop out flesh, holding oranges over a bowl to catch juice. Wrap orange shells in plastic wrap; refrigerate until needed.

2. Press orange pulp and juice through a sieve. Set aside. In a small saucepan, combine 1/4 cup sugar and water; bring to a boil, stirring until sugar dissolves. Boil 5 minutes; stir in juice mixture. Cool to room temperature.
3. Pour cooled orange mixture into a 9" x 5" loaf pan; freeze 2 hours or until partially frozen.
4. In a small bowl, beat egg white until soft peaks form. Gradually beat in 2 tablespoons sugar until stiff and glossy. Place partially frozen orange mixture in a medium bowl; beat until fluffy. Fold in egg-white mixture.
5. Spoon sorbet into loaf pan; freeze 2 hours or until frozen. Spoon mixture into reserved orange shells; serve immediately or freeze, tightly wrapped, up to 1 month. If frozen, place in refrigerator 30 minutes to soften before serving. Decorate with mint leaves. Makes 2 servings.

Left to right: Strawberry Ice, Amaretto Ice Bombe

Strawberry Ice

Granita di Fragole

1/2 cup sugar
1/4 cup water
1-1/2 cups fresh strawberries
2 tablespoons orange juice

1. In a small saucepan, heat sugar and water over low heat, stirring, until sugar dissolves. Increase heat; boil 5 minutes or until syrupy. Cool to room temperature.
2. Using a wooden spoon, press strawberries through a sieve into a medium bowl. Stir orange juice into sieved strawberries. Stir cooled syrup into strawberry mixture.

3. Pour strawberry mixture into a 9" x 5" loaf pan; freeze 3 to 4 hours or until firm. To serve, place in refrigerator 30 minutes to soften. Makes 2 servings.

Variations
Substitute thawed frozen strawberries for fresh ones.

Peach Ice (Granita di Pesche): Substitute 2 peeled and pitted, ripe medium peaches for strawberries. If peaches are very ripe, press through a sieve. If peaches are firm, process in a blender until pureed. Add peach puree to cooled sugar syrup; freeze as above.

1. In a small bowl, combine macaroon crumbs and liqueur. Dampen a 2-cup bowl or mold. Line base of bowl or mold with waxed paper. Freeze lined bowl or mold until chilled.

2. Press about 1/4 of ice cream over bottom of chilled bowl or mold. Spread with 1/2 of macaroon mixture. Spoon 1/2 of remaining ice cream over macaroon mixture. Spread remaining macaroon mixture over ice cream. Top with remaining ice cream. Freeze 1 hour or until firm.

3. To serve, remove bombe from freezer. In a small bowl, whip cream until stiff. Place a serving plate over bombe; invert. Loosen bombe with a knife, if necessary. Remove bowl or mold and waxed paper. Frost bombe with whipped cream.

4. Sprinkle top with crushed macaroon; freeze 15 minutes before serving if bombe has softened. Makes 2 servings.

Coffee Ice Cream

Gelato al Caffe

---

2 egg yolks
5 tablespoons sugar
1/2 cup milk
1/4 cup coffee beans
1/2 cup whipping cream

---

1. In a small bowl, beat egg yolks and sugar until lemon-colored. In a small saucepan, heat milk and coffee beans until simmering. Beat hot milk and coffee beans into egg-yolk mixture.

2. Place bowl over a pan of simmering water; cook, stirring, about 20 minutes or until custard is thickened.

3. Strain custard into a clean bowl; discard coffee beans. Place bowl with custard in a larger bowl of iced water. Stir occasionally until cooled to room temperature.

4. In a small bowl, whip cream until soft peaks form. Fold whipped cream into cooled custard. Pour mixture into a 9" x 5" loaf pan; freeze about 3 hours or until firm.

5. To serve, place ice cream in refrigerator 30 minutes to soften. Scoop into 2 dessert dishes. Makes 2 servings.

Amaretto Ice Bombe

Gelato all'Amaretto

1/4 cup Italian macaroon crumbs
2 tablespoons amaretto liqueur
1 cup vanilla ice cream

To serve:
1/2 cup whipping cream
1 macaroon, crushed

Choose a good quality, firm ice cream to make this bombe, or make your own vanilla ice cream. Substitute a vanilla bean for coffee beans, following recipe for Coffee Ice Cream, at right.

Chestnut Puree with Cream

Monte Bianco

3/4 cup canned chestnut puree (about 6 oz.)
2 tablespoons dark rum
1/4 cup powdered sugar

Topping:
1/4 cup whipping cream
1 teaspoon sugar
1 teaspoon dark rum

To decorate:
Semisweet chocolate, grated

Any leftover chestnut puree can be frozen for another use.

1. In a small bowl, beat chestnut puree until smooth. Beat in rum and powdered sugar. Spoon into 2 wine glasses or dessert dishes.
2. To make topping, in a small bowl, whip cream until soft peaks form. Beat in sugar and rum. Swirl whipped-cream mixture over chestnut mixture; refrigerate until served or up to 4 hours.
3. Decorate with grated chocolate. Makes 2 servings.

Zabaglione

Zabaglione Freddo

2 egg yolks
2 tablespoons sugar
1/3 cup Marsala
3 tablespoons whipping cream

To serve:
Italian macaroons or ladyfingers

---

1. In a small bowl, whisk egg yolks and sugar about 5 minutes or until foamy and lemon-colored. Whisk in Marsala; place bowl over a saucepan of barely simmering water.
2. Whisk zabaglione over simmering water 10 to 15 minutes or until it starts to thicken. Remove from saucepan; cool to room temperature, whisking occasionally.
3. In a small bowl, whip cream until soft peaks form. Fold whipped cream into cooled zabaglione. Spoon mixture into 2 wine glasses or dessert dishes. Refrigerate until chilled.
4. Serve with macaroons or ladyfingers. Makes 2 servings.

Mocha Mousse

Mousse Mocha

2 to 4 rose leaves
3 oz. semisweet chocolate, chopped
Vegetable oil
2 eggs, separated
2 tablespoons double-strength coffee
1/4 cup whipping cream
2 tablespoons sugar

To serve:
1/4 cup whipping cream

---

1. Gently wash rose leaves; pat dry with paper towels.
2. Melt chocolate in a very small saucepan over very low heat; stir until melted. Cool slightly.
3. Lightly brush shiny side of rose leaves with oil. Dip oiled side of each leaf into melted chocolate to completely cover. Do not get chocolate on unoiled side of leaves. Place leaves, chocolate-side up, on waxed paper until set.
4. Beat egg yolks and coffee into remaining chocolate until smooth; set aside. In a small bowl, whip cream until soft peaks form; beat in sugar. Fold whipped-cream mixture into chocolate mixture.
5. In a small bowl, beat egg whites until stiff but not dry. Fold beaten egg whites into chocolate mixture. Pour into a serving dish. Serve immediately or cover and refrigerate up to 24 hours.
6. To serve, peel leaves carefully from chocolate. Set aside. In a small bowl, whip cream until stiff peaks form. Spoon whipped cream into a pastry bag fitted with a large star tip. Pipe a star in center of mousse. Decorate with chocolate leaves. Makes 2 servings.

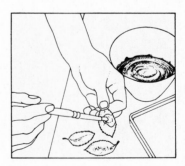
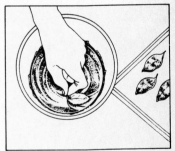
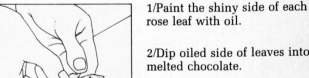

1/Paint the shiny side of each rose leaf with oil.

2/Dip oiled side of leaves into melted chocolate.

3/Peel leaves carefully from chocolate. Work quickly to prevent chocolate from melting.

Left to right: Chestnut Puree with Cream, Zabaglione, Mocha Mousse

Baked Peaches
with Macaroons

Pesche alla Piemontese

---

3 firm, ripe medium peaches, halved, pitted
1/2 cup Italian macaroon crumbs
2 tablespoons sugar
2 tablespoons butter or margarine, room temperature
1 egg yolk

Italian macaroons have a deliciously distinctive almond flavor. They are sold loose in boxes or wrapped in paper in twos. The paper-wrapped ones have the richest flavor.

1. Preheat oven to 350F (175C). Butter a shallow oven-proof dish large enough to hold peaches in 1 layer.
2. Scoop out about 1/2 inch of flesh from center of each peach half; place pieces from centers in a bowl. Add macaroon crumbs, sugar, butter or margarine and egg yolk to peach pieces; mash with a fork to combine.
3. Place peach halves, cut-side up, in buttered dish. Spoon a little macaroon mixture in center of each peach half.
4. Bake in preheated oven 25 to 30 minutes or until peaches are tender and filling is golden brown. Serve warm. Makes 2 servings.

Clockwise from left: Baked Peaches with Macaroons, Caramel Bread Pudding, Apricot Tart

Apricot Tart

Torta di Albicocche

Pastry:
3/4 cup all-purpose flour
1/4 cup butter or margarine
1/4 cup sugar
1 teaspoon grated lemon peel
1/8 teaspoon vanilla extract
1 egg yolk
1 teaspoon water

Filling:
6 to 8 fresh medium apricots, halved, pitted
1 tablespoon water
6 tablespoons sugar

---

1. To make pastry, place flour in a small bowl. With a pastry blender or 2 knives, cut in butter or margarine until mixture resembles coarse crumbs.
2. Stir in sugar and lemon peel. Stir in vanilla, egg yolk and water to form a firm dough. Shape into a ball; wrap in plastic wrap. Refrigerate 30 minutes.
3. Preheat oven to 400F (205C). To make filling, in a medium saucepan, combine apricots, water and 3 table-spoons sugar. Simmer 5 minutes or until apricots are beginning to soften. Cool slightly; drain well.
4. On a lightly floured surface, roll out dough to an 8-inch circle. Use pastry to line a 6-inch flan pan.
5. Arrange drained apricots in pastry-lined pan; sprinkle with remaining 3 tablespoons sugar.
6. Bake in preheated oven 25 to 30 minutes or until pastry is golden brown. Serve warm or at room temperature. Makes 2 servings.

How to Line a Flan Pan

To neatly line a flan pan, roll out pastry to a circle 2 inches larger than pan. Roll pastry circle around roll-ing pin. Beginning at edge of pan, unroll pastry onto flan pan. Without stretching, gently press dough into edges to prevent shrinking. Roll rolling pin firmly over flan pan to trim off excess pastry.

Caramel Bread Pudding

Budino di Pane Caramellato

---

5 tablespoons sugar
1 tablespoon water
1/3 cup dry bread crumbs
2 tablespoons butter or margarine
3 tablespoons raisins
3/4 cup milk
5 tablespoons sugar
1/4 cup pine nuts
2 tablespoons dark rum
2 eggs, separated

---

1. Preheat oven to 325F (165C). Lightly oil a 3-cup char-lotte pan or a round cake pan.
2. In a small heavy saucepan, combine 5 tablespoons sugar and water. Stir over low heat until sugar dissolves. Increase heat. Boil about 5 minutes, without stirring, or until caramel is golden brown. Remove from heat; pour into oiled pan, tilting to cover bottom evenly. Set aside.
3. Place bread crumbs, butter or margarine and raisins in a small bowl. In a small saucepan, bring milk to a boil; pour hot milk over crumb mixture. Stir until butter or margar-ine melts. Stir in 5 tablespoons sugar, nuts, rum and egg yolks until combined.
4. In a small bowl, beat egg whites until stiff but not dry. Fold beaten egg whites into crumb mixture. Pour into oiled pan; place in a baking pan. Add enough hot water to baking pan to fill halfway.
5. Bake in preheated oven about 1-1/4 hours or until firm to the touch and a knife inserted off center comes out clean. Remove from water; cool on a wire rack until just warm.
6. To remove from pan, loosen pudding with a knife. Place a serving place over pudding; invert. Remove pan. Serve warm or at room temperature. Refrigerate leftovers. Makes 2 servings.

Index